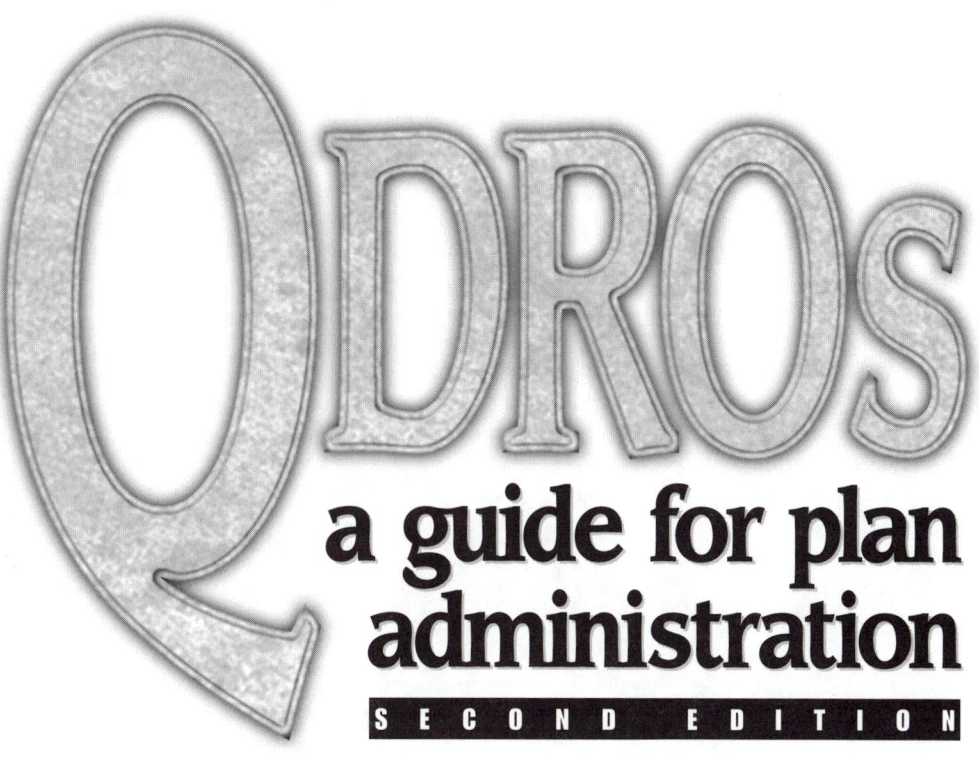

Julie L. Bloss, CEBS

QDROs
a guide for plan administration
SECOND EDITION

International Foundation of Employee Benefit Plans

The opinions expressed in this book are those of the author.
The International Foundation of Employee Benefit Plans disclaims
responsibility for views expressed and statements made in books
published by the Foundation.

> *This publication is designed to provide accurate and authoritative information in regard to the subject matter covered. It is sold with the understanding that the publisher is not engaged in rendering legal, accounting or other professional service. If legal advice or other expert assistance is required, the services of a competent professional person should be sought.*
>
> —*From a Declaration of Principles jointly adopted by a Committee of the American Bar Association and a Committee of Publishers and Associations.*

Edited by Mary Jo Brzezinski

Copies of this book can be obtained from:
  Publications Department
  International Foundation of Employee Benefit Plans
  18700 West Bluemound Road
  P.O. Box 69
  Brookfield, Wisconsin 53008-0069
  (414) 786-6710, ext. 8240

Payment must accompany order.
Call (888) 33-IFEBP for price information.

Published in 1997 by the International Foundation of Employee Benefit Plans, Inc.
©1997 International Foundation of Employee Benefit Plans, Inc.
All rights reserved.
Library of Congress Catalog Card Number: 97-70271
ISBN 0-89154-511-5
Printed in the United States of America

Dedication

To Brian, who understood when Mom
spent so many hours at her computer

Table of Contents

About the Author xi
Preface xiii

Chapter One . . . **What Is a QDRO?** 1
   Introduction 1
      Background 1
      Unanswered Questions for the DOL 2
      Treasury Guidance 3
      Definition of a *QDRO* 4
   QDROs and Various Types of Plans 4
      Welfare Benefit Plans 5
      Plans Subject to COBRA and QMCSOs 6
      Retirement Plans 7
   Plan Language 8
   Legal Requirements for Orders 9
      Domestic Relations Orders 9
      Alternate Payees 10
      Clearly Specifying Names and Mailing Addresses 11
      Other Requirements 12
      Benefit Payments 12
   QDRO Checklist 13
   Summary 14

Chapter Two . . . **Plan Administrators and Their Legal Obligations** 19
   Introduction 19
   Establishing Procedures 19
      Segregated Accounts 20
   Documenting Procedures 20

Releasing Information About the Plan	22
Privacy Concerns and Fiduciary Duties	22
Beneficiary Rights	23
Subpoenas	24
Two Participants	26
Information, Not Advice	26
Helpful Information	27
Valuation Issues	27
Burdensome Requests	28
The Interest of Potential Alternate Payees	28
Freezing Benefits	29
Schoonmaker	30
Releasing a Claim	31
Determining the Status of an Order	35
Sample Orders	35
Collecting Other Information	35
Tax Consequences of QDROs	36
QDROs May Shift Tax Burden	36
Other Tax Issues	38
Summary	39
Chapter Three . . . **Communicating About QDROs**	43
Approaches to Communication	43
Minimum Communication	43
More Efficient Communication	44
Communication Required by Law	45
Little Communication Required	46
Keeping Everyone in the Loop	46
Parties Without Lawyers	47
Samples	48
Optional Communication	53
Before an Order Is Drafted	53
Working With Attorneys	53
Sample Packet	55
Summary	67

Chapter Four . . . **Managing QDROs** 69
    Introduction 69
    Need for Management Procedures 69
    Restricting Distributions 70
    Organizing Paperwork 71
    Fees for QDROs 74
        Individual Fees 74
        Department of Labor Position 75
    Selecting and Training Personnel 76
    Simplifying Internal Communication 79
    Summary 84

Appendix 85
    Internal Revenue Code, Section 414(p), 26 U.S.C. §414(p) 85
    ERISA Section 206(d), 29 U.S.C. §1056(d) 90
    Treasury Regulation, Section 1.401(a)-13(g) 95
    Legislative History Retirement Equity Act, P.L. 98-397 98
    IRS Notice 97-11, Sample Language
        for a Qualified Domestic Relations Order 105
    Small Business Job Protection Act of 1996, H.R. 3448 122

Select Bibliography 125

Index 129

About the Author

Julie L. Bloss, CEBS, is a free-lance writer and an attorney for the Annuity Board of the Southern Baptist Convention in Dallas, Texas. She serves on the Governing Council of the International Society of Certified Employee Benefit Specialists (ISCEBS) and is past president of the Dallas/Fort Worth Chapter of the ISCEBS.

After graduating with a B.A. from Baylor University, Ms. Bloss received her law degree from Southern Methodist University (SMU). She has taught in the CEBS program at SMU and frequently speaks at conferences about employee benefits and legal issues. She is a former trustee of the Board of Pensions of the Presbyterian Church (USA) in Philadelphia.

Ms. Bloss has written hundreds of articles about legal topics and serves on the editorial boards of several publications. In 1991, she received the Individual Preventive Law Prize from the National Center for Preventive Law for a series of articles about legal issues affecting churches and nonprofit organizations.

She is the author of the first edition of *QDROs: A Guide for Plan Administration* (International Foundation of Employee Benefit Plans, 1991) and *The Church Guide to Employment Law* (Christian Ministry Resources, 1993).

Preface

When researching the first edition of this book in 1991, I found only a handful of court opinions mentioning qualified domestic relations orders (QDROs). Congress created QDROs with the Retirement Equity Act of 1984, but by 1991, few cases involving QDROs had worked their way through the courts. Nevertheless, divorce attorneys were drafting enough QDROs (or QDRO wannabes) to create headaches for plan administrators. I wrote the first edition to give plan administrators practical suggestions about how to manage the QDROs that came their way.

Six years later, there are hundreds, if not thousands, of reported court cases that refer to QDROs. Most of those cases do not involve "real" QDRO issues; that is, the cases usually don't address issues like whether an order met the statutory QDRO requirements or whether a plan administrator correctly interpreted a QDRO. Courts often mention QDROs when discussing some other contested aspect of a divorce. Sometimes courts refer to QDROs when describing the division of marital property. Sometimes opinions address whether a lower court correctly split a retirement account. Plan administrators generally are not interested in whether the participant or alternate payee got their fair share of the marital property or of a retirement account—plan administrators just want to be sure they approve and properly administer QDROs.

This second edition will discuss court cases and other guidance released after publication of the first edition. Like the first edition, this second edition will offer plan administrators practical suggestions for managing QDROs.

These practical suggestions are now more important than ever. Downsizing, right-sizing and reengineering are the buzzwords of the nineties. With budget cuts and staff reductions, pension plan administrators increasingly need efficient systems for managing their duties.

Since publication of the first edition, the Department of Labor (DOL) has taken the position that plan administrators cannot charge fees to individual participants for processing QDROs. To make matters worse, many plan administrators now have to cope with the evil twin of QDROs, qualified medical child support orders, or QMCSOs, sometimes known as "kiddie QDROs." Although QDROs and QMCSOs share some characteristics, QMCSOs are different animals, which this author will gratefully leave to some other writer.

Six years ago, plan administrators needed comprehensive DOL guidance about QDROs. Although the DOL is working on that guidance, plan administrators still don't have it. Six years ago, plan administrators complained about the orders they received from attorneys. Six years later, they are still complaining. *"Plus ça change, plus c'est la même chose"* (the more things change, the more they remain the same).

Julie L. Bloss, CEBS

Introduction

ONE OF THE FUNDAMENTAL PRINCIPLES OF PENSION LAW IS that plan benefits cannot be assigned or alienated. Like the first edition of *QDROs: A Guide for Plan Administration*, this second edition focuses on an important exception to that rule, the exception for qualified domestic relations orders (QDROs).

Background

QDROs were created when Congress passed the Retirement Equity Act of 1984[1] (REA), which amended the Employee Retirement Income Security Act of 1974[2] (ERISA) and the Internal Revenue Code[3] (the Code). Both ERISA and the Code prohibit the assignment or alienation of plan benefits.[4] Prior to REA, some plan administrators wound up in court when they refused to honor divorce decrees purporting to assign benefits from a participant to a participant's former spouse. Various courts disagreed on the issue of whether plan benefits could be assigned to a former spouse as part of a divorce settlement.[5]

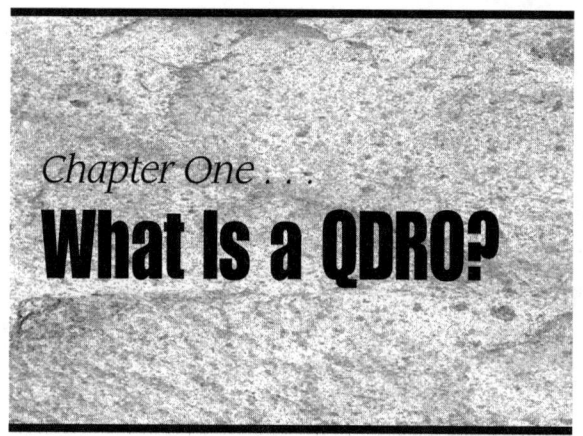
Chapter One...
What Is a QDRO?

REA settled that question by establishing the QDRO rules, which tell plan administrators when they must honor a court order directing the assignment of benefits to the former spouse of a plan participant. Unfortunately, however, although the law is clear that plan administrators should honor QDROs to assign plan benefits, the law is not clear about many aspects of QDRO administration. One commentator has observed that, although the QDRO requirements seem clear, "[i]n practice, many plan administrators find the

QDRO requirements complicated and incomplete."[6] Another attorney has characterized them as "maddeningly incomplete."[7]

Unanswered Questions for the DOL

Although more than six years have passed since publication of the first edition of this book, plan administrators still have no regulations to which they can turn for guidance as they approve and administer QDROs. But despite this lack of guidance, plan administrators are receiving more orders to approve every year.[8] In October of 1993, the Department of Labor (DOL) asked interested parties such as plan administrators for comments about whether the DOL should issue QDRO regulations and the issues those regulations should address.

The magnitude of the regulatory task is illustrated by a 37-page report submitted by Thomas Terry, chair of the American Bar Association's (ABA's) Section on Taxation.[9] The report, written by the Section of Taxation's Committee on Employee Benefits, reflected the individual views of those members.[10] The report responded to the following five issues the DOL had raised when it asked for comments:[11]

- ❏ Whether and to what extent, state or federal law applies to issues arising under the QDRO provisions
- ❏ Whether fiduciary or other problems have arisen relating to the plan administrator's duties, including providing information to participants and alternate payees; determining whether a DRO is a QDRO; making the determination during a "reasonable" period; protecting the plan from adverse consequences, such as double payments; and administering divided plan benefits
- ❏ Whether problems have arisen in interpreting ERISA Section 206(d)(3) to determine the qualified status of a DRO
- ❏ Whether problems have arisen relating to the ERISA Section 206(d)(3)(G) and (H) process for determining the status of a DRO and interim administration of the plan and benefits
- ❏ Whether problems have arisen in determining whether rights and benefits granted to an alternate payee under a QDRO or pursuant to plan provisions are consistent with ERISA and the Code.

By March 1997, the DOL had drafted a booklet offering guidance about QDROs; however, that booklet had not been cleared for publication at the time this book went to press. Regulations could be years away.

Treasury Guidance

While the DOL worked on its own guidance, Congress gave specific instructions to the Secretary of the Treasury in the Small Business Job Protection Act of 1996 (SBJPA): Develop sample language for inclusion in a form for a QDRO that meets the requirements of ERISA and the Internal Revenue Code no later than January 1, 1997.[12] That law also requires the Secretary of the Treasury to include publicity about the sample language in its pension outreach efforts.[13]

In response to the SBJPA, the IRS issued Notice 97-11 in December 1996 to provide "information intended to assist domestic relations attorneys, plan participants, spouses and former spouses of participants, and plan administrators in drafting and reviewing . . ." QDROs. The appendix attached to the notice included sample QDRO language and a discussion. The DOL, which has jurisdiction to interpret QDRO provisions in ERISA paralleling those in the Code, affirmed that the IRS and Treasury discussion and sample language are "consistent with the views of the Department of Labor concerning the statutory requirements for QDROs." The text of the notice and the appendix are reprinted on pages 105-121 in the appendix of this book.

Unfortunately, Notice 97-11 didn't tell plan administrators much. Or as one commentator said, it was "pretty basic."[14]

Notice 97-11 reviews the statutory requirements for QDROs and describes the difference between defined benefit and defined contribution plans. Although this discussion may not help many plan administrators directly, it could be helpful to divorce attorneys who are not familiar with the basic QDRO rules. If a plan administrator has absolutely no general information to send to divorce attorneys who want basic information about QDROs, the plan administrator could provide a copy of Notice 97-11.

Nevertheless, Notice 97-11 will never be as helpful as a packet of information about a particular plan's QDRO requirements. The notice warns that QDROs must conform to plan terms and that the sample language is merely a sample. A valid QDRO doesn't have to use the sample language, and some of the sample language may be inappropriate for some plans. Also, the sample language includes some information that is not required by the law.

Although Notice 97-11 reviews some factors to consider when a QDRO assigns the amount or percentage of benefits to be assigned to an alternate payee, the appendix gives no sample language. The notice says that's due to the "complexity and variety of the factors that should be considered." Nevertheless, the notice encourages drafters to consider issues relevant to defined benefit and defined contribution plans. If nothing else, the notice should convince divorce attorneys that there is no such thing as a one-size-fits-all QDRO and that plan administrators are not being petty when they refuse to accept an order that other plan administrators accepted in the past.

Definition of a *QDRO*

What is a QDRO? Here is a simple definition: A *QDRO* is a special court order that permits a plan administrator to assign benefits from a plan participant to another person who is usually the participant's former spouse or child. As one might expect from ERISA and the Code, however, the legal definition of a QDRO is much longer and more technical.

QDROs are usually a byproduct of divorce. Divorces may involve a number of professionals, including attorneys, accountants and therapists. Divorcing couples usually pay for the services of those professionals. But divorces increasingly involve employee benefits professionals—the plan administrators who process QDROs.

These plan administrators may spend hours on QDRO issues. Unlike other professionals involved in a divorce, they don't get paid by the divorcing couple for their work. Yet plan administrators wear many hats when they work with QDROs. As one author has observed, "It is somewhat ironic that the more a plan administrator knows about QDROs, the more difficult is the administrator's multifaceted position: as neutral advisor to attorneys drafting QDROs, as judge of the qualified status of DROs and as administrator of the distributions ordered."[15]

Plan administrators have several important concerns about QDROs. First, plan administrators need to be able to answer the question: "What is a QDRO?" In other words, they must be able to identify an order that meets the statutory definition of a QDRO in order to fulfill their fiduciary responsibilities to plan participants. Second, they need to understand their legal obligations to the parties involved with QDROs. Next, plan administrators need to understand how to communicate information about QDROs to plan participants, alternate payees and their attorneys. Finally, plan administrators need a system for managing QDROs.

This chapter will help plan administrators answer the question: "What is a QDRO?" The remaining chapters will address other QDRO issues.

QDROs and Various Types of Plans

QDROs may affect qualified pension, profit-sharing and stock bonus plans.[16] More specifically, the QDRO rules do not apply to plans to which Section 401(a)(13) of the Internal Revenue Code does not apply.[17] Nevertheless, distributions from 403(b) plans pursuant to a QDRO are treated the same way as distributions from plans to which 401(a)(13) applies.[18]

Welfare Benefit Plans

The first edition of this book stated unequivocally that welfare benefit plans such as group insurance programs are not affected by the QDRO rules,[19] and that is still the opinion of this author. Code Section 414(p)(9) clearly states that Section 414(p) does not apply to any plan to which Section 401(a)(13) does not apply.[20] Section 401(a)(13) does not apply to welfare benefit plans;[21] therefore, the QDRO rules should not apply to welfare benefit plans.

Nevertheless, in 1994 a federal court held that the QDRO rules apply to benefits from an employer's group life insurance plan.[22] *Metropolitan Life v. Wheaton* is a troublesome case and has been criticized for its conclusion.[23] The *Metropolitan Life* case arose when the children of a deceased General Electric employee tried to claim employer-provided life insurance benefits.[24] The employee had gotten a divorce about a year before he died.[25] The divorce decree had ordered him to name his two minor children as beneficiaries of his employer-provided life insurance.[26] When the employee remarried, he named his new wife as his beneficiary.[27] When he died, his widow and his children both claimed the benefit.[28]

The Seventh Circuit Court of Appeals held that the QDRO rules applied to the life insurance plan.[29] The court also found that the divorce decree ordering the employee to name his children as beneficiaries was a QDRO.[30] The court reached this conclusion by what it called a literal reading of ERISA as amended by the Retirement Equity Act.[31]

The court noted that QDROs are an exception to ERISA's antialienation rules.[32] The court recognized that ERISA's antialienation rules apply only to pension plans.[33] But the court also examined ERISA's preemption provisions and noted that they apply to both pension and welfare benefit plans.[34]

After closely examining the Retirement Equity Act and an alternate payee's rights to payments under a plan,[35] the court decided that the QDRO rules applied not only to pension plans but to welfare plans as well.[36] Commentators have suggested that the court's reasoning was flawed.[37] The court ignored Section 206(d)(3)(L) of ERISA (which does not relate to welfare plans) and thus "neglected an important provision that provides additional guidance with respect to the meaning of a *plan* to which the QDRO rules can apply."[38]

The *Metropolitan Life* court observed that an "employee's life insurance will often be as important to the survivors as his pension benefits."[39] According to the court, it did not make sense to permit retirement benefits, but not welfare benefits, to be assigned.[40] The court offered this justification for its decision: If a QDRO can override a beneficiary designation in a pension plan, why wouldn't Congress allow a QDRO to do the same thing in a welfare plan?[41] That's an interesting question, but REA's legislative history refers only to pension benefits.[42] The legislative history does not suggest that Congress ever thought about applying QDRO rules to welfare benefit plans.[43]

After deciding that the QDRO rules applied to welfare benefit plans, the court held that the divorce decree in this case, which required the employee to name his children as beneficiaries of his life insurance, was a QDRO.[44] The court reached this conclusion despite the widow's argument that the order did not meet ERISA's requirements for a QDRO.[45] For example, the order did not include the specific name of the plan nor did it give the children's addresses.[46] The order also did not say how the insurance was to be divided between the two children.[47]

Had a similar order been presented to a pension plan administrator, almost undoubtedly the plan administrator would have refused to honor it as a QDRO.[48] Apparently the Seventh Circuit is not as picky as most plan administrators. The court said: "It is asking too much of domestic relations lawyers and judges to expect them to dot every *i* and cross every *t* in formulating divorce decrees that have ERISA implications."[49] Divorce attorneys could read the court's decision as saying "close" is good enough in horseshoes and in QDROs.

When finding that the QDRO rules applied to welfare plans, the court based its ruling on what it called a literal reading of ERISA.[50] Then it basically decided that the QDRO rules do not need to be taken literally.[51] This case is troublesome for plan administrators in the Seventh Circuit, and it will be troublesome for plan administrators in other circuits if other courts follow the Seventh Circuit's lead.

Plans Subject to COBRA and QMCSOs

Employees and their spouses may understandably be confused about the laws that affect employee benefits after divorce. Former spouses of employees with employer-sponsored group insurance programs may have rights to continued medical coverage under the federal Consolidated Omnibus Budget Reconciliation Act [52](COBRA) or under various state laws.[53] Employees and their spouses are increasingly aware of their COBRA rights. COBRA may be a familiar term to many employees, but QDRO is not.

Similarly, employees are becoming more familiar with qualified medical child support orders (QMCSOs),[54] sometimes known as "kiddie QDROs." These orders require an employer to permit the children of a divorced employee to continue medical insurance coverage after a divorce. Both COBRA and QMCSOs are outside the scope of this book. Nevertheless, plan administrators need to remember that plan participants, their former spouses and their attorneys may understandably get confused about QDROs, COBRA and QMCSOs, all of which may need to be addressed at the time of divorce.[55]

Retirement Plans

Because most participants and their dependents recognize their current need for medical insurance coverage, they will probably be quite concerned about how divorce will affect their coverage. That's an issue they will probably discuss with their employer or insurance carrier before the divorce is final. Unfortunately, parties to a divorce and their attorneys are not always as diligent about addressing how the divorce will affect pension benefits, particularly if the parties are a long way from retirement. Even when a court enters an order about a retirement account, the plan administrator may not find out about it for years.

Most plan administrators have had the frustrating experience of suddenly receiving a copy of a ten-year-old order attempting to assign pension benefits when the plan administrator wasn't even aware that the participant had gotten a divorce. These old orders surface from time to time as if neither the participant nor the alternate payee thought it was worth the time to apprise the plan administrator of the divorce. Plan administrators can approve old orders as QDROs; however, plan administrators can't do anything if the participant has taken some action in the interim to reduce the alternate payee's rights to benefits. Clients can't always rely on their attorneys to send an order to the plan administrator for approval as a QDRO, and this is one thing that may fall through the cracks when the divorce is finalized. This author wonders how some divorce attorneys have avoided malpractice claims[56] in situations where they forget to send an order to the plan administrator for approval as a QDRO.

When plan administrators restrict distributions from an account because of a claim from a potential alternate payee, they need to be sure that the restriction doesn't remain indefinitely. Plan administrators may therefore want

What Is a QDRO?

to contact parties they haven't heard from at least every 12 months to find out what has happened. Sometimes these reminder letters will flush out a QDRO, or sometimes they may remind the parties to tell the plan administrator that they have reconciled or that the participant retained all rights to the retirement account after divorce. The reminder letters should advise prior claimants that the plan administrator will not continue to restrict distributions unless the claimant reasserts rights to the account in writing by a certain deadline.

Clearly, plan administrators may have a special challenge in focusing the parties' attention on the QDRO rules. The type of plan and the size and nature of the plan administrator will affect the plan administrator's QDRO procedures, forms and communication materials. The sample letters, forms and procedures in this book are generic so they can be used with different types of plans. As a practical matter, plan administrators need to develop their own procedures, forms and communication materials tailored to their particular plans and plan participants.

Plan Language

All qualified plans must contain a provision prohibiting the assignment or alienation of benefits,[57] but the QDRO rules create an exception to this general prohibition.[58] Although plans will not lose their qualified status if they are not amended to mention the QDRO rules,[59] a well-written plan document should refer to them. Plan language about QDROs does not need to set out the QDRO rules in their entirety, nor does it need to describe the plan administrator's procedures for determining the status of an order.

This sample plan language could follow plan provisions prohibiting the assignment or alienation of plan benefits:

> The preceding paragraph prohibiting the assignment or alienation of benefits does not apply to a domestic relations order which is determined by the plan administrator to be a *qualified domestic relations order (QDRO)* as defined by Section 414(p) of the Internal Revenue Code. The plan administrator will establish written procedures to determine whether domestic relations orders are qualified and to administer distributions under these orders.

Similar language could appear in a question and answer format in a summary plan description (SPD):

> *Are participants' benefits subject to the claims of creditors?* As a general rule, a participant's benefits cannot be garnished, alienated, transferred or assigned to creditors, either voluntarily or involuntarily. This

rule does not apply if the plan administrator determines that a domestic relations order is a qualified domestic relations order (QDRO) as defined by Section 414(p) of the Internal Revenue Code.

Legal Requirements for Orders

QDROs and QDRO wannabes come in various flavors, and plan administrators have seen them all. Some are included in property settlement agreements, and some are found in divorce decrees. Others are found in stand-alone orders. Some are relatively short and avoid much legalese, to the extent it is possible to avoid legalese in a court order governed by ERISA and the Code. Others are long documents with page after page of boilerplate language that some divorce attorneys add to every QDRO they draft. But the style of a QDRO is not important—it's the substance that counts. Long or short, simple or complex, these orders must meet certain statutory requirements to be treated as QDROs.

Domestic Relations Orders

Only *domestic relations orders (DROs)* may be treated as QDROs.[60] *Domestic relations orders* include judgments, decrees or orders,[61] all of which are legal documents signed by a judge. A property settlement agreement between a couple is not a DRO unless it has been approved by a court.[62] Plan administrators should not recognize informal or voluntary agreements between divorcing couples attempting to assign pension benefits—a court order is essential.

Participants and their former spouses may be very frustrated by the requirement that a judge has to sign an order about a retirement account before the plan administrator will consider assigning a benefit. The former spouse, in particular, may think that the plan administrator is merely being recalcitrant. Nevertheless, the law is clear that without a DRO, there can be no QDRO.

Although federal law establishes the QDRO rules, divorce and the division of marital property are governed by the laws of each individual state. Judges generally have a great deal of discretion in determining how marital assets are divided. Even in community property states, plan benefits will not necessarily be divided equally. In order to be treated as a QDRO, a domestic relations order must be made pursuant to state domestic relations law, including community property law.[63] Accordingly, an ordinary creditor cannot obtain a QDRO because the order would not be made pursuant to a state domestic relations law.

According to the DOL, plan administrators should not review state court orders for correct application of state marital property law or for fairness.[64] They merely need to focus on whether the order is a QDRO.[65] The DOL took this position when a plan administrator was presented with a state court order annulling a marriage of 38 years that had produced six children.[66]

Plaintiffs have attempted to have court orders treated as QDROs in some interesting cases. In one case, a court held that a plan participant's daughter could not show that a judgment she got against her father for physical and sexual abuse was a QDRO.[67] In another case, a deceased employee's disabled adult child brought suit under ERISA when he was denied death benefits from his father's retirement plan.[68] In that case, the court concluded that the plan's committee had not made an arbitrary or capricious decision when it determined that a 1966 divorce decree was not a QDRO and did not award benefits to the disabled child.[69]

Alternate Payees

The domestic relations order must relate to child support, alimony or marital property rights of an "alternate payee."[70] An *alternate payee* may be the plan participant's spouse, former spouse, child or other dependent who is given a right to all or part of the participant's benefits in the court order.[71] Most QDROs assign benefits to a former spouse at the time of divorce even if that person is not entitled to an immediate distribution. As divorcing couples increasingly focus on employer-provided benefits, plan administrators will have to deal with more questions about pensions.[72]

Divorcing couples may mistakenly think of pension plans like savings accounts or IRAs, particularly if the participant has a defined contribution plan. Participants and their spouses may assume they can tap their retirement benefits in an emergency, and most couples consider a divorce to be an emergency. Often one spouse wants to "cash out" his or her pension benefits to buy a house or otherwise start a new life. In these cases, the plan administrator may have the challenge of explaining why the plan does not offer ready access to cash.

When pension benefits are the largest marital asset, they are more likely to be subject to a QDRO. On the other hand, if the couple has additional assets, the spouse may be more willing to trade an interest in the participant's retirement benefits for cash or some other asset. Clearly, however, trading assets so that the participant retains all of his or her interest in a pension plan is not a viable option for many couples. If it were, there would be no need for the QDRO rules.

When the participant is not eligible for an immediate distribution from a plan at the time of divorce, it is unlikely that a QDRO will be entered for the purpose of providing child support. But if a participant is already receiving regular benefit payments from a plan and if the couple has minor children, a QDRO is more likely to relate to child support. If child support payments get significantly in arrears, a QDRO could be entered sometime after the divorce to satisfy those obligations.

Divorce decrees may require one parent to make child support payments to a state agency. The state agency then pays the other parent. A plan administrator should be able to make payments to such an agency without violating the terms of a QDRO.[73] Although the plan's payments may be directed to the agency, the alternate payee really gets the benefit of the payments. Legislative history therefore suggests that for tax purposes, the alternate payee is in constructive receipt of the payments.[74] Nevertheless, distributions to a non-spouse alternate payee are included in the participant's gross income.[75]

Clearly Specifying Names and Mailing Addresses

In addition to relating to the rights of an alternate payee, domestic relations orders must meet some other requirements before they can be treated as QDROs. The order must *clearly specify* the name and last known mailing address (if any) of both the plan participant and the alternate payee.[76]

According to the legislative history of the statute:

An order will not be treated as failing to be a qualified order merely because the order does not specify the current mailing address of the participant and alternate payee if the plan administrator has reason to know that address independently of the order. For example, if the plan administrator is aware that the alternate payee is also a participant under the plan, and the plan records include a current address for each participant, the plan administrator may not treat the order as failing to qualify.[77]

In *Shelstead v. Shelstead,* a California court held that an order was not a QDRO because it failed the "clear specification" requirement.[78] The plan had been ordered to pay a share of a participant's pension benefits to his former wife "or her designated successor in interest" until the participant's death, if the former wife died before the participant.[79] The court rejected a number of arguments made by the plan about why the order was not a QDRO; however, it accepted the plan's argument that the order did not "clearly specify" who was to receive the benefits.[80] That's because the plan would have too many uncertainties about its obligations to the former wife's "successor."[81]

The court sent the case back to the lower court so the parties could modify the order by a certain date and turn it into a QDRO.[82] The former wife would be permitted to name a successor; however, that person would have to be identified with more specificity.[83] Also, the higher court reversed the award of attorney fees that the lower court had imposed on the plan.[84]

Other Requirements

To be a QDRO, the order must clearly specify the amount or percentage of the benefit to be paid to the alternate payee or the manner of determining the amount or percentage.[85] Also, the order must set forth the number of payments or time period to which the order applies.[86] Finally, the order must clearly specify each plan to which it applies.[87] General references to "the pension plan of XYZ Corporation" or to "retirement benefits from participant's employment with XYZ Corporation" are not sufficient.[88]

Benefit Payments

Even if a domestic relations order meets all of the requirements discussed previously, it could contain some provisions that would disqualify it from being treated as a QDRO. A QDRO cannot require the plan to provide any type or form of benefit or payment option unless the plan itself provides for the same form of benefit or payment option.[89] Despite this requirement, a QDRO may order payments to an alternate payee on or after the date on which the participant attains or would have attained the "earliest retirement age" under the plan, even if the participant has not yet separated from service.[90] *Earliest retirement age* is defined as the earlier of: (1) the date on which the participant is entitled to a distribution; or (2) the later of the date the participant reaches age 50 or the earliest date on which the participant could begin receiving benefits if the participant separated from service.[91]

A QDRO can require payments to an alternate payee as if the participant had retired on the date the payment is to begin.[92] In that case, the present value of accrued benefits would be taken into account, but the present value of employer subsidies for early retirement would not be considered.[93] In determining the present value, the interest rate specified in the plan is used.[94] If no interest rate is specified in the plan, 5% is used.[95]

A QDRO may require the payment of benefits to the alternate payee in any form the plan permits the participant to be paid, other than in the form of a joint and survivor annuity for the alternate payee and the alternate payee's subsequent spouse.[96] Nevertheless, a QDRO cannot require the plan to provide increased benefits that are determined on the basis of actuarial value.[97] Finally, a QDRO cannot require payment of benefits to another alternate payee if the plan has an obligation to pay another alternate payee because of an earlier QDRO.[98]

A QDRO may contain provisions relating to the survivor benefits of the alternate payee. In some cases, the alternate payee may have survivor benefits greater than those of a participant's subsequent spouse. For example, the QDRO can order that the former spouse (and not any subsequent spouse to whom the participant is married at the participant's death) be treated as the survivor of the participant for purposes of the joint and survivor annuity and preretirement survivor annuity rules of Section 401(a)(11) and the minimum survivor annuity requirements of Section 417.[99]

QDRO Checklist

Checklists can simplify the review process for plan administrators.[100] Plan administrators may find it difficult to remember all of the QDRO rules when reviewing domestic relations orders. That's why a QDRO checklist is essential. Just as the most experienced pilot never takes off without reviewing a written list of procedures, a plan administrator should never approve an order as a QDRO without completing a checklist. Plan administrators who are not attorneys can use checklists to reduce the time and money spent on legal fees by identifying defective orders instead of sending them for immediate review by attorneys.[101]

The following questions should be answered "yes" before the plan administrator treats an order as a QDRO:

☑ 1. Is the order a domestic relations order?

An order is a *domestic relations order* if it is a judgment, decree, order or approval of a property settlement that:

- Relates to the provision of child support, alimony payments or marital property rights to a spouse (present or former), child or other dependent of a plan participant and

- Is made pursuant to a state domestic relations law, including a community property law.

Note: A property settlement agreement that has not been approved by a court is not a domestic relations order.

What Is a QDRO?

☑ 2. Does the order contain the name and last known mailing address of the participant?

☑ 3. Does the order contain the name and last known mailing address of each alternate payee covered by the order?

> *Note: If the plan administrator has reason to know the participant's or alternate payee's address independently of the order, the order does not fail to qualify merely because a current mailing address is not included.*

☑ 4. Does the order create or recognize the rights of one or more alternate payees (other than the participant) to receive all or part of the participant's plan benefits?

> *Alternate payee* is defined as any spouse, former spouse, child or other dependent.

☑ 5. Does the order specify the amount or percentage of the participant's benefits to be paid by the plan to each alternate payee, or the manner in which such amount or percentage is to be determined?

☑ 6. Does the order specify the number of payments or the period to which such order applies?

☑ 7. Does the order contain the name of the plan(s) to which it applies?

☑ 8. Does the order provide benefits at a time or in a form that is available under the plan document?

☑ 9. Does the order only require the plan to provide benefits that do not exceed the participant's plan benefits?

☑ 10. Does the order refrain from affecting any benefits of a prior known QDRO?

Summary

In summary, plan administrators should be familiar with ERISA and the Code so they can identify QDROs. An order that's called a QDRO isn't always a QDRO. It's up to the plan administrator to decide if an order is a QDRO. As discussed in the next chapter, plan administrators must develop procedures for reviewing orders and helping them meet their legal obligations in processing and administering QDROs.

Endnotes

1. Retirement Equity Act of 1984, Pub. L. No. 98-397 (codified as amended in scattered sections of 26 and 29 U.S.C.A.). The legislative history of the QDRO provisions in REA is reprinted in the appendix.
2. The current version of ERISA begins at 29 U.S.C. §1001. ERISA's most important provisions about QDROs are reprinted in the appendix. For clarity, future citations to ERISA will omit the reference to the United States Code (U.S.C.). Although ERISA and the IRC have similar provisions about QDROs, most citations will be given to the IRC only.
3. The current version of the Internal Revenue Code of 1986 (IRC) begins at 26 U.S.C.A. §1 (West Supp. 1996). The IRC's most important provisions about QDROs are reprinted in the appendix. For clarity, future citations to the IRC will omit the reference to the United States Code Annotated (U.S.C.A.). Although the IRC and ERISA have similar provisions about QDROs, most citations will be given to the IRC only.
4. ERISA §206(d)(1); IRC §401(a)(13)(A).
5. See, e.g., *American Tel. & Tel. Co. v. Murray*, 592 F.2d 118 (2d Cir. 1979); *Weir v. Weir*, 173 N.J. Super. 130, 413 A.2d 638 (1980).
6. Richardson, "Qualified Domestic Relations Orders: Navigating the Cross Fire," 11 *Compensation & Benefits*, 48, 50 (1995).
7. Meyer, "Qualified Domestic Relations Orders: What the Statute Doesn't Say," 7 *Benefits Law Journal*, 311, 312 (1994).
8. Murtha, "Divorce Is Hard on Benefits Managers," 12 *Crain's New York Business*, 22 (June 17, 1996).
9. Reprinted in *Highlights & Documents*, 3439 (March 3, 1995).
10. *Id.*
11. *Id.* at 3439-40.
12. Pub. L. No. 104-188, §1457, 110 Stat. 1755, 1818-19 (1996).
13. *Id.* at 1819.
14. Boutwell, "Practical Advice on QDRO Quagmire," *Panel Publishers 401(k) Advisor*, 2 (March 1997).
15. Drinkwater, "Qualified Domestic Relations Orders," *Employee Benefits Practices*, 1, 1 (Third Quarter 1990).
16. See IRC §414(p)(9).
17. IRC §414(p)(9).
18. *Id.*
19. J. Bloss, *QDROs: A Guide for Plan Administration*, at 2 (1991).
20. IRC §414(p)(9).
21. IRC §401(a) relates to qualified pension, profit-sharing and stock bonus plans.
22. *Metropolitan Life v. Wheaton*, 42 F.3d 1080 (7th Cir. 1994).
23. Dodge and Morris, "QDROs and Welfare Benefit Plans After *Metropolitan Life v. Wheaton*," 8 *Benefits Law Journal*, 43, 45 (1995). See also *Hawkins v. Commissioner*, 20 Employee Benefit Cas. (BNA) 1513, 1522 (10th Cir. 1996) (criticizing the court's conclusion in *Metropolitan Life* that the order contained the provisions required by IRC §414(p)). *Hawkins* is further discussed in Chapter Two.
24. 42 F.3d at 1082.

25. *Id.* at 1081-82.
26. *Id.* at 1081.
27. *Id.* at 1081-82.
28. *Id.* at 1082.
29. *Id.* at 1084.
30. *Id.* at 1085.
31. *Id.* at 1084.
32. *Id.* at 1082.
33. *Id.* at 1083.
34. *Id.*
35. *Id.*
36. *Id.*
37. *Dodge & Morris, supra*, at 47.
38. *Id.*
39. 42 F.3d at 1083.
40. *Id.*
41. *Id.*
42. The legislative history of the Retirement Equity Act, P.L. 98-397, is found in the appendix.
43. See *id.*
44. 42 F.3d at 1085.
45. *Id.* at 1084.
46. *Id.*
47. *Id.*
48. See *Dodge and Morris, supra*, at 47.
49. 42 F.3d at 1085.
50. *Id.* at 1084.
51. See *id.*
52. The COBRA continuation of coverage rules begin at ERISA §601 and IRC §4980B.
53. E.g., Tex. Ins. Code Ann. art. 3.51-6 §3B (Vernon Supp. 1996).
54. ERISA §609.
55. For general information about various types of benefits which may be impacted by divorce, see MacMillan and Nebel, "The Dilemmas of Divorce," 73 *HRFOCUS*, 11 (1996).
56. For a discussion of pitfalls for non-ERISA attorneys working with retirement benefits, see Brucker and Hiltunen, "The Firm Beware: When Non-ERISA Professionals Advise on Retirement Matters," 2 *Journal of Pension Benefits*, 80 (1995).
57. ERISA §206(d)(1); IRC §401(a)(13)(A).
58. ERISA §206(d)(3)(A); IRC §401(a)(13)(B).
59. Treas. Reg. §1.401(a)-(13)(g)(2) (as amended in 1988).
60. IRC §414(p)(1)(A).
61. IRC §414(p)(1)(B).
62. *Id.*
63. IRC §414(p)(1)(B)(ii).
64. DOL Advisory Op. 92-17A.
65. *Id.*
66. *Id.*

67. *Mills v. Mills*, 790 F.Supp. 172 (S.D. Ohio 1992).
68. *Barnes v. Maytag Corporation*, 799 F.Supp. 926 (S.D. Ill. 1992).
69. *Id.* at 932.
70. IRC §414(p)(1)(B)(i).
71. IRC §414(p)(8).
72. MacMillan and Nebel, *supra*, at 11 (1996).
73. H.R. Rep. No. 526, 99th Cong., 2d Sess., pt. 2, at 27 (1986).
74. *Id.*
75. IRS Notice 89-25, Q & A-3.
76. IRC §414(p)(2)(A).
77. S. Rep. No. 575, 98th Cong., 2d Sess. 20 (1984). *Stinner v. Stinner*, 554 A.2d 45, 48 (Pa.), *cert. denied*, 492 U.S. 919 (1989).
78. 58 Cal. Rptr. 2d 522 (Cal. Ct. App. 1996).
79. *Id.* at 525.
80. *Id.* at 531.
81. *Id.*
82. *Id.*
83. *Id.*
84. *Id.* at 532.
85. IRC §414(p)(2)(B).
86. IRC §414(p)(2)(C).
87. IRC §414(p)(2)(D).
88. Potter, "How to Draft a Qualified Domestic Relations Order," 1 *Journal of Taxation of Employee Benefits*, 250, 251 (1994).
89. IRC §414(p)(3)(A).
90. IRC §414(p)(4)(A)(i).
91. IRC §414(p)(4)(B).
92. IRC §414(p)(4)(A)(ii).
93. *Id.*
94. IRC §414(P)(4)(A).
95. *Id.*
96. IRC §414(P)(4)(A)(iii).
97. IRC §414(p)(3)(B).
98. IRC §414(p)(3)(C).
99. IRC §414(p)(5)(A). For additional information about the effect of QDROs on survivor benefits, see Treas. Reg. §1.401(a)-(13)(g), which is reprinted in the appendix.
100. Smith, "When Is a DRO a QDRO?" 19 *Employee Benefits Journal*, 37, 42 (1994).
101. "A 12-Point Checklist to Weigh the Legitimacy of Your QDRO Claims," 94-4 *IOMA's Report on Managing 401(k) Plans*, 2, 3 (1994).

Introduction

AS DISCUSSED IN CHAPTER ONE, PLAN ADMINISTRATORS must be able to judge whether a DRO is a QDRO. Orders must meet a number of legal requirements before they can be treated as QDROs. These requirements place a burden on the attorney drafting the order. But the law also places some burdens on the plan administrator, the most important of which is deciding whether a DRO meets the requirements of ERISA and the Code and can be treated as a QDRO.

Establishing Procedures

Chapter Two . . .
Plan Administrators and Their Legal Obligations

Plans must establish "reasonable" procedures for determining whether an order is a QDRO and for administering payments under the order.[1] Because *reasonable* is not defined, plan administrators have some flexibility in developing procedures. QDRO procedures are discussed in more detail later in this chapter.

Whenever a plan administrator receives a DRO, the plan administrator must "promptly" notify the participant and alternate payee(s) that the order has been received.[2] Additionally, the plan administrator must "promptly" notify the participant and alternate payee(s) of the plan's procedures for determining whether a domestic relations order is qualified.[3] *Promptly* is not defined, but as discussed in Chapter Three, plan administrators can use form letters and memos for quicker and more efficient correspondence with participants and alternate payees.

Within a "reasonable" period after receiving the order, the plan administrator must determine if the order is a QDRO and must advise the participant and the alternate payee(s) of that determination.[4] *Reasonable is* not defined, so plan administrators should be able to establish timetables that work for them.[5] Although *reasonable* and *promptly* aren't defined, some practitioners have suggested that it's not a good idea to have bright line rules for these terms.[6] They prefer a facts and circumstances test, which gives plan administrators flexibility and may enable them to more easily work out difficulties with participants and alternate payees.[7]

Segregated Accounts

Additional rules apply to plan administrators when the status of an order is being determined. During that time, the plan administrator must separately account for amounts that would be payable to the alternate payee if the order were determined to be a QDRO.[8] These funds for which the plan administrator must separately account are called *segregated amounts*.[9]

If the plan administrator determines that an order is a QDRO within 18 months, the segregated amounts, including interest, must be assigned.[10] The 18-month period begins on the date on which the order would require the first payment to be made.[11] If an order is not determined to be a QDRO or if the question of whether it is a QDRO is not resolved within 18 months, the plan administrator is supposed to pay the amounts to the "person or persons who would have been entitled to such amounts if there had been no order."[12]

Documenting Procedures

As discussed above, plans are required to establish reasonable procedures for determining the status of domestic relations orders and for administering distributions under them.[13] These procedures can be a "good offense" for plan administrators to show that the plan complied with the law.[14] The law does not specify the format for these procedures nor does it indicate where these procedures should be located. Most plan administrators will avoid including their QDRO procedures in plan documents because the procedures may be changed periodically. One alternative is to set out QDRO procedures in the summary plan description (SPD); however, the procedures may change too often for this to be a viable alternative. Moreover, plan administrators may not want to lengthen SPDs with these procedures.

Many plan administrators will opt to include QDRO procedures where other administrative issues are addressed, perhaps in plan rules in an administrative manual. Administrative manuals should be easier and less expensive to update than plan documents or SPDs. The following sample language may be used in an administrative manual to describe a plan's procedures for determining if an order is a QDRO.

Qualified Domestic Relations Order Procedures for XYZ Pension Plan

When XYZ Pension Plan receives a domestic relations order, the following procedures will be used to determine whether it is a qualified domestic relations order (QDRO) under the Employee Retirement Income Security Act of 1974 (ERISA) and the Internal Revenue Code (IRC).

1. The plan will separately account for the amounts that appear to be awarded to an alternate payee. If the participant is already receiving a benefit, the portion of the benefit that appears to be awarded to the alternate payee will be suspended.

2. The order will be referred to XYZ's Legal Department for review and a determination of its status. That determination will be made 45 days after receipt of the order or within any time period that may be established by federal regulations in the future.

3. The plan will promptly notify the participant and any potential alternate payee in writing that the order has been received by the plan and has been referred to the Legal Department for a determination of its status within 45 days. Potential alternate payees will be identified by the plan administrator before the order is sent to the legal department. Potential alternate payees are generally the spouse or former spouse of a participant but may be the child or any other dependent the order indicates has an interest in the benefits affected by the order.

4. After the plan's attorney determines the status of an order, the plan administrator will promptly notify the participant and alternate payee(s) of the determination in writing. If the order has been determined to be a QDRO, the assignment will be made.

5. The participant may continue to direct investments in the account until an order is approved as a QDRO.

Plan Administrators and Their Legal Obligations

> **QDRO Procedures—Continued**
>
> 6. If the plan's attorney determines that an order is not a QDRO, the plan will not make any distributions from the participant's account if the potential alternate payee notifies the plan administrator in writing within three weeks of receipt of the notice of rejection of the order that another order is being sought to correct the deficiencies in the defective order. If the participant is already receiving a benefit, the portion of the benefit that appears to be awarded to the alternate payee will continue to be suspended if the potential alternate payee notifies the plan administrator in writing within three weeks of receipt of the notice of rejection that another order is being sought to correct the deficiencies in the defective order. Nevertheless, if 12 months pass without any communication from the parties or the attorneys about the status of the new order, the plan will no longer suspend benefits or separately account for them.

Releasing Information About the Plan

To obtain reliable information about plan benefits, attorneys should seek information directly from the plan administrator. Before contacting the plan administrator, the attorney may already have obtained some general information about the plan from the participant or spouse. Because most employees do not understand their own pensions,[15] the initial information they give to their attorneys may be obsolete, erroneous or incomplete. The attorney representing the participant's spouse may assume that the participant is deliberately trying to cloud information about the plan. In many cases, however, the participant truly does not know much about the plan, and his or her spouse knows even less.

Privacy Concerns and Fiduciary Duties

Although attorneys need current information about plan benefits so they can draft QDROs, plan administrators have concerns about their fiduciary duties and the privacy of plan participants. That's why plan administrators may decide not to disclose information about benefits to attorneys or to spouses without a subpoena or the participant's written consent. A sample consent form is included in Chapter Three on page 66 as part of a package of divorce information.

Some attorneys would argue that a spouse or former spouse is automatically entitled to information about the value of retirement benefits that may be considered marital assets under state law. But as discussed below, the QDRO rules in ERISA and the Code do not specifically require plan administrators to disclose account information to a spouse or former spouse unless that person is an alternate payee.[16] Section 105(a) of ERISA requires plan administrators to furnish information about total benefits accrued "to any plan participant or beneficiary" who requests this information in writing;[17] however, the plan administrator does not have to provide it more than once every 12 months.[18]

Beneficiary Rights

Is a spouse or other *potential* alternate payee a *beneficiary* who is entitled to receive information about a participant's account? The DOL hasn't issued guidance on that point. According to ERISA, however, an *alternate payee* is a beneficiary under the plan.[19] This provision strongly suggests that an individual does not have rights as a beneficiary until a DRO is approved as a QDRO; that is, when a potential alternate payee actually becomes an alternate payee. Nevertheless, one could argue that if the potential alternate payee is the spouse of a participant, he or she has rights as a potential plan beneficiary because of the joint and survivor rules.[20] Arguably, a spouse or former spouse of a participant who is already receiving benefits under a QJSA would have a stronger claim to being a beneficiary than the spouse or former spouse of a participant whose benefits are not in pay status.[21]

Even if a former spouse doesn't become a beneficiary under ERISA until actually becoming an alternate payee, that person could still assert ERISA rights for actions the plan took before the former spouse became an alternate payee. In *Lynn v. Lynn*, a court held that a former wife was a "beneficiary" under a "QDRO" and therefore had standing to assert claims under ERISA although a court order concerning the pension plan had not yet been presented to the plan administrator for approval.[22] In that case, a court had ordered the husband to pay $50,000 of the wife's attorney fees.[23] The husband appealed that order, but three months later, his appeal was denied and he was ordered to withdraw $44,000 from his retirement account to pay the attorney fees.[24] The plan had been established some years before for the husband's wholly owned corporation.[25] Between the time the first order was entered and the appeal was denied, the husband, as trustee of the plan, had the plan amended to prevent any distributions.[26]

The wife filed suit in federal court alleging a violation of ERISA because she had been discriminated against in exercising her rights under the plan.[27] The lower court found that the plan amendments were valid.[28] Moreover, the lower court said the former wife was not an alternate payee at the time the discriminatory acts allegedly took place and therefore was not a beneficiary with standing to assert ERISA claims.[29]

The Fifth Circuit Court of Appeals disagreed, concluding that "Mrs. Lynn is precisely the sort of claimant who Congress intended to protect. . . ."[30] According to the Fifth Circuit, the husband's actions came "perilously close to a sham" on both the divorce court and the federal system of protecting pension benefits.[31] The lower court had held that Mrs. Lynn became an alternate payee under a QDRO issued with the final divorce decree months after the plan was amended.[32] In other words, the lower court had found that Mrs. Lynn became an alternate payee and therefore a beneficiary under the plan after Mr. Lynn amended the plan, so she had no rights at the time the plan was amended.[33]

The Fifth Circuit said that Mrs. Lynn had rights under ERISA the moment she became an alternate payee and felt the effects of the discriminatory action, even though that discriminatory action had been taken before she became an alternate payee.[34] The court used this illustration:

> This case is analogous to the situation of a mad terrorist who plants a time bomb in a school, which explodes after ten years, killing a classroom full of second-graders. Although none of the lives existed at the time the bomber placed the explosives, once the bomb detonates, the crime is no less murder.[35]

In this case, the court clearly objected to manipulation of plan provisions to enable the participant to circumvent the rights of a potential alternate payee. One could envision a similar situation in which a participant withdrew funds without his former spouse's consent while an order dividing a retirement account was on appeal. The participant could argue that spousal consent was unnecessary because the divorce was final and there was no valid QDRO presented to the plan administrator. As illustrated by the *Lynn* opinion, however, a court could find that as soon as the appeal ended, making the former spouse an alternate payee, the alternate payee could assert her ERISA rights for the plan's action in permitting the distribution.

Subpoenas

A subpoena to release information about the plan should not be required by a plan administrator unless the participant refuses to sign a consent form. Often participants will agree to sign a consent form when they learn that their spouse is going to get the same information as soon as a subpoena can be obtained.

Unfortunately, some attorneys routinely serve subpoenas on plan administrators without first contacting the plan administrator to determine if there is another way to get information about the participant's benefits. When a participant is willing to consent voluntarily to the release of information, a subpoena is a wasted extra expense. Moreover, subpoenas may be overly broad because they are not tailored to the particular plan and its participants. These "fishing expedition" subpoenas mean more work for the plan administrator who may have to search records for extremely old information or who may have to explain to the attorney why some questions are irrelevant, redundant or seek information the plan administrator does not have.

Often subpoenas are not addressed to a specific person at the plan administrator's office. Employees therefore need to be trained about where to forward the subpoena for a response. Subpoenas should be directed to the appropriate person immediately. Subpoenas should be reviewed by legal counsel even if counsel will rely on a nonlawyer to collect most of the requested information.

Subpoenas require information to be returned by a certain date, and a plan administrator that fails to file a response on time could find itself subject to judicial sanctions. If special circumstances prevent a timely response, a plan administrator should get the attorney to agree to extend the deadline. Additionally, the plan administrator should be able to convince an attorney that some of the requested information is irrelevant. For example, a plan administrator of a defined contribution plan may receive a subpoena referring to benefit formulas applicable only to defined benefit plans. Plan administrators should be able to work out these differences with attorneys over the phone. Telephone conversations can then be documented with a memo to the file or in a letter to the attorney confirming the conversation.

In some cases, a plan administrator may be subpoenaed to give a deposition or testimony in court about the plan benefits at issue. Most plan administrators want to avoid the time and expense involved in depositions or court appearances. They therefore have a real incentive to cooperate with attorneys seeking information about the plan. A subpoena may direct a plan administrator to appear in court or at an attorney's office at a specific date and time to produce relevant records. A plan administrator can often convince an attorney that a personal appearance is not necessary if the plan administrator is willing to send the records to the attorney prior to the time of appearance shown on the subpoena. If an attorney and plan administrator agree to this arrangement in a telephone conversation, the plan administrator should confirm the agreement in a letter to the attorney.

Two Participants

When releasing plan information, plan administrators should check to see whether the participant's spouse or former spouse is also a plan participant. Particularly in the case of large employers in small towns, it is not unusual for a couple to have the same employer and therefore participate in some of the same employee benefit plans. When a divorce is pending, the lower paid spouse may seek to establish a right to benefits from plans in which the higher paid spouse participates. Plan administrators need to know if both parties participate in the same plan so they can provide complete and accurate benefit information. If both spouses are plan participants, the QDRO should refer to the benefits available to each party. This approach will help reduce confusion about both parties' future rights to benefits.

Information, Not Advice

Neither ERISA nor the IRC imposes a duty on plan administrators to assist participants, alternate payees or their attorneys in preparing QDROs. Attorneys who cooperate with and get good information from plan administrators are more likely to prepare QDROs acceptable to plan administrators; however, plan administrators should *never*, under any circumstances, give legal advice. Plan administrators who provide helpful information to attorneys upfront are less likely to receive defective orders that require time-consuming contact with attorneys and their unhappy clients about defects and how they can be corrected. As further discussed in Chapter Three, some plan administrators save time by providing attorneys with sample QDROs that meet the plan's requirements but that can be modified to meet the objectives of the parties.

Regardless of how much information they provide, plan administrators should remain neutral and avoid getting involved in disputes between the parties. For example, the plan administrator should not decide how much of the benefits, if any, should be payable to a participant's former spouse or to any other alternate payee. Once that decision is made by the parties, their attorneys and ultimately a judge, the plan administrator can provide appropriate guidance about how to implement that decision with a QDRO. If a plan administrator is advised that the parties intend to divide the benefits in half, the plan administrator is not giving legal advice or taking sides by providing a sample QDRO or by telling the attorneys how to word an order to assign half of the benefits.

Helpful Information

When releasing information about a plan to attorneys and their clients, plan administrators should begin with the assumption that the people receiving the information know absolutely nothing about the plan. Like other professionals, plan administrators have their own lingo, which is often completely meaningless to other people. A plan administrator supplying information to an attorney preparing a QDRO should start with the basics. Instead of immediately discussing the assumptions used in projecting a benefit payable from a "DB" plan or the specific provisions of a "k" plan, the plan administrator should first briefly explain what a defined benefit plan is or how a 401(k) plan works.

As discussed above, plan administrators should be able to convince attorneys that sometimes the information they want is not applicable to the participant's plan. For example, questions about benefit formulas may be irrelevant to defined contribution plans. On the other hand, if the participant has consented to the release of information or if a valid subpoena has been issued, the plan administrator may volunteer information that may not be asked about directly but that could have a substantial impact on the QDRO. When attorneys know very little about a plan, they have to play a guessing game about which questions they should ask. Full disclosure of relevant information makes the entire QDRO process more efficient and less time-consuming. Nevertheless, when providing information, plan administrators should not lose sight of their fiduciary responsibility to plan participants.

Valuation Issues

Providing information to couples and their attorneys about the value of defined benefit plans can be particularly time-consuming and therefore expensive for plan administrators. Sometimes attorneys will request information about the value of benefits under various assumptions without realizing that these requests can involve time-consuming actuarial calculations. Administrators of defined benefit plans have some alternatives for dealing with attorneys who demand too much information. First, they may want to limit the number of times they provide information about the value of plan benefits if actuarial calculations are involved. Alternatively, they may want to impose a fee for additional benefit projections. If the attorneys want more projections, they can hire their own actuaries. In fact, a court may ultimately have to determine whose expert has correctly valued the disputed benefits.[36]

Burdensome Requests

A plan administrator should be able to limit the number of benefit projections it is willing to make even if a subpoena is served. A subpoena requires production of documents or information in the possession of the person or entity served. If a plan administrator has not already made a benefit projection using the assumptions set forth in the subpoena, the plan administrator can truthfully respond that such information is not in its possession. Likewise, plan administrators should be able to avoid other unduly burdensome demands for information even if those demands appear in a subpoena.

If an attorney goes to the trouble of getting a subpoena served, he or she will probably ask for everything but the kitchen sink. A plan administrator's phone call or letter may help the attorney understand that the lawyer really does not need everything listed in the subpoena. For example, a subpoena could ask for information about the amount and dates of contributions made to a defined contribution plan for the last 25 years. The plan administrator may be able to educate the attorney that this information is not necessary for drafting a valid QDRO. As discussed above, concessions made by the attorney in a telephone conversation should be documented in writing, either in a memo to the file or in a letter from the plan administrator. If the attorney will not agree to modify a subpoena voluntarily, a plan administrator should not hesitate to avail itself of any legal remedies to avoid burdensome requests.

The Interest of Potential Alternate Payees

As further discussed in Chapters Three and Four, plan administrators usually find it helpful to communicate with attorneys representing divorcing parties prior to the time the final order is signed by the judge. Of course, the plan administrator may not know a divorce is pending until a final order has already been entered. Some attorneys will obtain a restraining order against the plan. Legislative history of the Tax Reform Act of 1986 says that plans can honor these restraining orders.[37] Particularly in California divorces, the plan may be joined in the divorce proceedings to prevent plan assets from being disbursed to the participant before a QDRO can be prepared.

Freezing Benefits

In most cases, the qualified joint and survivor annuity (QJSA) rules offer some protection to a spouse who would otherwise lose all benefits if a participant could receive a distribution without spousal consent.[38] When those rules apply, the participant can only receive a QJSA unless the spouse agrees otherwise. Nevertheless, when a potential alternate payee has made a claim to retirement benefits, the plan administrator should be extremely careful about making distributions or setting up a benefit.

Any former spouse who thinks he or she will be protected by survivor benefit rules should obtain a QDRO while there are still survivor rights to protect. In *Hopkins v. AT&T Global Information Solutions Inc.*, a court held that a current wife's interests in her husband's pension plan vested when he retired.[39] Therefore, the wife to whom he was married at the time of retirement, not the wife who obtained a QDRO after his retirement, was entitled to survivor benefits.

When Mr. and Mrs. Hopkins divorced in 1986, Mr. Hopkins' retirement benefits were listed as a marital asset; however, Mrs. Hopkins wasn't awarded part of it. Mr. Hopkins remarried after the divorce, and his first wife got a court order attaching his wages so that she could collect current and past-due alimony. After Mr. Hopkins retired, his ex-wife could no longer attach his wages. In 1994, she got a judgment of over $15,000 for past-due alimony, and she attempted to get a QDRO so she could collect it.

A court subsequently entered two orders. One ordered monthly payments to Mr. Hopkins' ex-wife from his pension benefits, and the other ordered payments from the surviving spouse benefits. The plan administrator agreed that it could treat the first order as a QDRO; however, it argued that because the surviving spouse benefits had already vested in the second wife, it couldn't honor the second order.

The Fourth Circuit Court of Appeals agreed with the plan administrator. According to the court, the wife to whom Mr. Hopkins was married at the time of retirement was a "beneficiary" under ERISA, not a "participant." But to be "qualified," a domestic relations order has to relate to a participant's benefit. The court noted that a former spouse who wants surviving spouse benefits should obtain a QDRO before the participant retires.

Plan administrators frequently receive letters from attorneys representing spouses of participants who are asserting a marital property claim to plan benefits and who are demanding that no distributions be made until the spouse has an opportunity to establish this claim in court. As a precaution, the plan administrator may adopt procedures prohibiting distributions until the spouse releases the claim or until some other point in the QDRO process. Once a plan administrator receives an order to review, the plan administrator must separately account for any amounts that would otherwise appear to be payable to an alternate payee.[40]

Plan procedures may require benefits or accounts to be held or frozen while a DRO is being prepared.[41] Some plans may prefer to freeze accounts or benefits only when they get a DRO.[42] Plans may require the participant to sign a statement that no QDRO is being prepared if the plan has previously been made aware of a pending divorce and the participant then requests a distribution.[43] Despite what the plan decides to do about freezing accounts, that decision should be clearly specified in the plan's QDRO procedures and should be communicated to the parties.[44]

Schoonmaker

A federal court recognized plans' needs to freeze accounts prior to approval of an order as a QDRO in *Schoonmaker v. Employee Savings Plan of Amoco Corp.*[45] In that case, the court found that the plan had violated its written procedures by putting a hold on the account when it learned that a QDRO was being sent to the plan, because the plan's written procedures said that a hold would be placed on an account only while it was determining if a DRO it had received was a QDRO.[46] The participant learned of the hold on his account when the plan did not permit him to sell stock in his account shortly before the value of the stock dropped, causing him a significant loss.[47] The court recognized that what the plan did was reasonable because the hold was designed to protect beneficiaries and the plan.[48] Unfortunately for the plan, however, its written QDRO procedures didn't reflect the reasonable approach it actually took.[49] The court concluded that the plan had not breached its fiduciary duty,[50] which would have made damages against the plan even higher.

Because divorce proceedings can take years, the *Schoonmaker* court reached a practical conclusion when it decided that plan administrators could freeze accounts prior to receipt of a QDRO. If plan administrators wait to freeze distributions until a QDRO has been approved, the participant may be able to take action that would thwart the purpose of the QDRO. The plan administrator's duty is to the participant; however, as discussed above, there is some controversy about the plan administrator's duty to the alternate payee, the party that some people view as a beneficiary under the plan.

If a plan administrator knows of a spouse's claim and allows the plan participant to exercise all of his or her rights under the plan to the detriment of the potential alternate payee, the plan administrator shouldn't be surprised to be threatened with litigation. Plans therefore need to decide at what point in the QDRO process they will freeze benefits. And the lesson of *Schoonmaker* is that plan administrators must follow their written procedures, no matter how reasonable their actual practices may be.[51]

Releasing a Claim

A spouse may want to release a claim to retirement benefits if the couple reconciles. Sometimes a spouse who has asserted a claim to retirement benefits will want to release the claim before the divorce is final. If, for example, the participant is otherwise entitled to a distribution, the spouse may prefer for the participant to go ahead and receive the money and pay the spouse part of it rather than waiting for other issues relating to the division of marital property to be resolved by a final divorce decree. If a spouse wants to release a claim, the best protection for a plan administrator is a formal release in addition to any forms the parties would ordinarily sign to receive a distribution.

When a couple agrees to permit a participant to receive a distribution prior to entry of a divorce decree in order to pay the spouse, the parties may have to be reminded that the plan administrator cannot issue a separate check to the spouse without a QDRO. The spouse may want the participant to receive a check before the divorce is final without waiting for a QDRO; however, the spouse may not trust the participant to divide it as agreed. The spouse may therefore prefer that the check, made payable to the participant, be sent to an attorney's office. In that case, the parties can go to the bank together or make some other arrangement to ensure that the spouse gets paid. Although plan administrators should remain neutral, most plan administrators would prefer to accommodate requests for sending the check to a different address in lieu of receiving and reviewing QDROs.

The following forms can be used when a spouse wants to release a claim prior to approval of a QDRO.

> **NOTE:** The following letter and release may be used by plan administrators when a spouse wants to release a claim to a retirement account before a DRO is accepted as a QDRO by the plan administrator.

Mrs. Mary Doe
1234 Main Street
Anywhere, ST 00000

Re: Retirement account of John Doe
    Account number 55987

Dear Mrs. Doe:

Thank you for letting us know that you have agreed for Mr. Doe to receive a complete distribution from his retirement account before your divorce is final [or because you have decided not to seek an amended order acceptable to the plan as a QDRO].

As we explained when you first contacted us about your divorce, we cannot issue a separate check to you without a qualified domestic relations order (QDRO) that meets the requirements of Section 414(p) of the Internal Revenue Code. As previously agreed by both attorneys, after Mr. Doe completes the appropriate forms, we can mail the check payable to him to his attorney. You and your attorney can make your own arrangements about how you will receive your share of that check. We cannot be responsible if for some reason you do not receive a payment from Mr. Doe.

In addition to the forms Mr. Doe will have to complete, enclosed is a form for you to sign consenting to this distribution. Please return the forms to my attention so that we can process the distribution.

Very truly yours,

Jane Smith, CEBS
Benefits Administrator

cc: John Doe

NOTE: The following release can be used when a spouse wants to consent to a distribution to a participant while a divorce is still pending.

Release of Claim to Retirement Account
(Distribution During Divorce)

I, _____, for and in consideration of XYZ Corporation (XYZ) permitting a distribution of the retirement benefits of _____ ("the participant") (account no. _____) that are eligible for distribution pursuant to the plan in which s/he is a participant, hereby release and hold harmless XYZ from any and all liability arising out of XYZ's actions in making this distribution. I understand that once this distribution is made, XYZ will not be able to assist me in any effort to establish rights to these retirement benefits.

XYZ has made no representations about the tax consequences of this distribution. I further acknowledge that XYZ has not made any representations about the advisability of permitting the participant to take this distribution or about my rights to these benefits under any state law which may be applicable to this divorce proceeding. In consideration of XYZ processing this distribution, I agree to indemnify and hold harmless XYZ from any loss or damage that might arise by virtue of XYZ making this distribution. I further agree to pay all legal fees and court costs in the event XYZ is made a party to any lawsuit or other legal proceeding concerning this distribution.

Witness my hand this _____ day of _____, 19____.

Signature: _____
Name (print): _____
Social Security No.: _____
Date of Birth: _____
Address: _____
   _____
   _____

STATE OF _____
COUNTY OF _____

Before me, the undersigned notary, personally appeared _____, known to me, or proved to me on the basis of satisfactory evidence, to be the person whose name is subscribed to the foregoing instrument, and acknowledged to me that s/he executed the same for the purposes and consideration therein expressed.

GIVEN UNDER MY HAND AND SEAL OF OFFICE, this _____ day of 19____.

(Seal)
Notary Public in and for: _____
Name (print): _____
My commission expires: _____

This release must be completed in addition to any distribution forms required by XYZ Corporation.

Plan Administrators and Their Legal Obligations

NOTE: The following release can be used if a spouse wants to release a claim to a retirement account when no immediate distribution is anticipated.

Release of Claim to Retirement Account

I, _____, hereby release any and all claims to_____'s ("the participant's") retirement benefits (account no._____) from XYZ Corporation (XYZ). I understand that after I sign this release, the participant can exercise any and all rights under the plan.

XYZ has made no representations about the advisability of releasing a claim to this retirement account, nor has XYZ given me any advice about the marital property laws of any state that may affect my rights to this account.

I agree to indemnify and hold harmless XYZ from any loss or damage that may arise due to this release. I further agree to pay all legal fees and court costs in the event XYZ is made a party to any lawsuit or other legal proceeding concerning this release.

Witness my hand this _____ day of _____, 19____.

Signature: _____
Name (print): _____
Social Security No.: _____
Date of Birth: _____
Address: _____
_____
_____

STATE OF _____
COUNTY OF _____

Before me, the undersigned notary, personally appeared _____, known to me, or proved to me on the basis of satisfactory evidence, to be the person whose name is subscribed to the foregoing instrument, and acknowledged to me that s/he executed the same for the purposes and consideration therein expressed.

GIVEN UNDER MY HAND AND SEAL OF OFFICE, this _____day of 19___.

_____

(Seal)
Notary Public in and for: _____
Name (print): _____
My commission expires: _____

Determining the Status of an Order

Although the law requires plan administrators to determine whether a domestic relations order is a QDRO,[52] the statutes are not clear about who is to make this determination on behalf of the plan administrator. Arguably, the plan's legal counsel should decide this issue because the decision involves reviewing a legal document and determining whether that document complies with the law. Regardless of who makes the final decision, a checklist helps ensure that orders meet all the requirements of the law. Chapter One includes a checklist on pages 13 and 14 and so does Chapter Three's sample communication package to attorneys on page 62.

Sample Orders

Despite the plan administrator's duty to determine if an order is a QDRO and to pay benefits as directed by a court, the plan administrator should *never* attempt to give advice to the participant, the participant's spouse, former spouse or any attorneys about the amount that should be assigned. As discussed above, that issue must ultimately be decided by a court. Once a decision has been made about how much will be assigned, the plan administrator can supply the language to accomplish the objectives of the order. Sample or model orders are effective ways to communicate what a plan needs in a QDRO. When attorneys use standard language from a sample QDRO provided by a plan administrator, the plan administrator can determine the status of a DRO much more quickly than when the plan administrator gets a long DRO with pages of unfamiliar language. Chapter Three includes additional information about sample orders and an example of a sample QDRO.

Collecting Other Information

In their sample orders, plan administrators may want to solicit information that is not required by law for a valid QDRO but which would nevertheless be helpful to the plan administrator in processing the QDRO and in paying benefits affected by the QDRO. For example, the sample QDRO in Chapter Three asks for the Social Security numbers of both the participant and the alternate payee. This will help plans that keep records by Social Security numbers and will provide information for reporting future distributions to the IRS. Plan administrators may also want the birth dates of both the participant and the alternate payee. The birth dates may be helpful if the plan administrator has to perform any actuarial calculations relating to the benefit and for making required distributions.

Of course, there is no legal requirement for either Social Security numbers or birth dates to be included in a QDRO. Therefore, a plan administrator should not fail to qualify a DRO as a QDRO in the event this information is left out. As a practical matter, the plan administrator should already have the birth date and Social Security number of the participant, and often of the alternate payee. The alternate payee or his or her attorney should be willing to provide this information in a letter if it is not included in a QDRO. If the plan administrator has trouble getting this information from the alternate payee or the alternate payee's attorney, the plan administrator could encourage some action with a letter explaining that the information is important to ensure that the plan properly administers the alternate payee's rights under the QDRO.

Tax Consequences of QDROs

Although plan administrators may have opinions about the tax consequences of an assignment of plan benefits, they should refrain from giving tax advice to either the participant or the potential alternate payee. The plan administrator cannot possibly know how the division of the couple's other marital property will affect their tax situation, but more importantly, the plan administrator's duty is to administer the plan, not to give legal or tax advice. The plan administrator is therefore not in a position to evaluate the tax impact of a QDRO. A detailed discussion of the tax consequences of QDROs is outside the scope of this book; however, plan administrators should have some general knowledge about these issues.

QDROs May Shift Tax Burden

The question of whether a divorce decree or property settlement agreement is a QDRO can have significant tax consequences for the parties.[53] Generally, plan participants must pay taxes on distributions,[54] but a QDRO can shift that responsibility to an alternate payee.[55] If there is a dispute about whether an order is a QDRO, the resolution of that dispute could determine who pays taxes on a plan distribution.

Hawkins v. Commissioner[56] involved such a dispute. In that case, the parties' marital settlement agreement said that Mrs. Hawkins would immediately receive a $1 million distribution from Mr. Hawkins' pension plan, and that she would pay taxes on that amount.[57] She received the distribution but didn't roll it over, and neither one of them reported the distribution on their income tax returns.[58] Two years later, Mr. Hawkins asked the divorce court to enter a QDRO retroactively because the parties had intended for their settlement agreement to be a QDRO.[59] The divorce court refused, and the IRS subsequently ordered both parties to pay taxes on the $1 million distribution.[60]

Mrs. Hawkins argued that the order was not a QDRO, and the Tax Court agreed with her.[61] The Tax Court therefore concluded that Mr. Hawkins was responsible for taxes on the entire distribution, notwithstanding the fact that Mrs. Hawkins had gotten all the money.[62] On appeal, however, the Tenth Circuit held that the agreement was a QDRO and that Mr. Hawkins was therefore not responsible for the taxes on the distribution.[63] The Tenth Circuit said the settlement agreement was a QDRO because it satisfied the basic statutory requirements for a QDRO.[64] According to the court, an order can be a QDRO even if it does not track the specific language of the law.[65] For example, the court said that Mrs. Hawkins was an alternate payee under the agreement even though the order didn't call her that.[66] The court also said the order didn't fail as a QDRO merely because it didn't mention the alternate payee's last known mailing address.[67] Although the court ultimately decided that the order was a QDRO, a lot of litigation and money could have been saved if the order had tracked the statutory language.

In *Karem v. Commissioner*, the Tax Court held that a state court judgment partitioning martial property, including a retirement plan, was not a QDRO.[68] The Karems divorced in 1985 but did not divide their community property until 1988.[69] In 1987, Mr. Karem, with Mrs. Karem's consent, took a lump-sum distribution from his pension plan which he then deposited into his attorney's trust account to be held until the couple partitioned their community property.[70]

When the court entered a consent judgment partitioning the Karem's community property in 1988, the order said that Mrs. Karem would receive her interest in Mr. Karem's pension plan in the form of a monthly benefit pursuant to a QDRO to be prepared by Mr. Karem.[71] The order also said that she would get half of the money in the trust account.[72] Mr. Karem reported half of the distribution on his 1987 tax return, but the IRS argued that he should have reported all of it.[73] The Tax Court agreed with the IRS.[74] The Tax Court concluded that the judgment itself wasn't a QDRO because it was entered a year after the distribution.[75] According to the Tax Court, Section 414(p) requires a plan administrator to qualify an order as a QDRO *before* the plan makes a distribution to a spouse or former spouse.[76] The court also found that Louisiana community property laws did not make Mrs. Karem liable for taxes on half of the distribution; therefore, Mr. Karem was responsible for taxes on the entire amount.[77]

Burton v. Commissioner[78] involved another tax dispute over a distribution prior to entry of a QDRO. In that case, the divorce decree ordered Mr. Burton to withdraw all of his pension benefits, use them to pay off the mortgage on the family home and then pay any remaining benefits to his former wife. The divorce decree also stated that Mr. Burton was liable for all of the taxes due on the distribution and that he released his former spouse from any tax liability relating to the distribution.

After Mr. Burton paid off the mortgage and paid $30,000 to Mrs. Burton pursuant to the terms of the decree, he claimed an alimony deduction on his tax return for those payments.

After the IRS disallowed that deduction, Mr. Burton asserted that he was not liable for taxes on the distribution because the divorce decree was a QDRO.

Finding that the facts of the case didn't meet the requirements of Section 414(p), the Tax Court rejected Mr. Burton's argument that the divorce decree was a QDRO. The court noted that Mr. Burton himself received the distributions before the date of the decree so "it cannot be argued that the distribution was made by the plan administrator to an alternate payee...." The court observed that the divorce decree had never been presented to the plan administrator for approval as a QDRO.

Other Tax Issues

Tax considerations often play a significant role in how couples agree to divide marital property after divorce. Attorneys can creatively use QDROs to maximize their clients' tax benefits as they transfer marital property. For example, a participant who would otherwise be subject to the 15% penalty tax on excess distributions from a plan[79] may benefit from transferring some plan assets to a former spouse while retaining other assets.

Distributions for child support payments made to a state agency pursuant to a QDRO are included in the gross income of the alternate payee;[80] however, distributions to nonspouse alternate payees, like minor children, are includable in the participant's gross income.[81] Generally, plan administrators should withhold amounts from distributions to nonspouse alternate payees as if the participant were the payee.[82] Nevertheless, the plan must give the participant the opportunity to make a withholding election, and the participant may elect no withholding.[83]

An alternate payee who is a participant's former spouse and who receives an eligible rollover distribution may roll over the distribution.[84] Eligible rollover distributions to alternate payees are therefore usually subject to mandatory 20% withholding if the alternate payee does not directly roll over the distribution.[85] If the distribution is not an eligible rollover distribution, or if the alternate payee decides not to roll over an eligible rollover distribution, the alternate payee is generally subject to the same tax rules as the participant.[86] Distributions to nonspouse alternate payees are not eligible rollover distributions and are not subject to the mandatory 20% withholding requirements.[87] All of these rules may come as a surprise to an alternate payee, who, for whatever reason, may not realize that a distribution from a pension plan can come with hefty tax consequences.

Distributions to participants before age 59½ are usually subject to a 10% penalty,[88] but distributions to alternate payees are not subject to this penalty.[89] The ages of the alternate payee and participant don't matter—a 24-year-old alternate payee will not have to pay the 10% penalty for a distribution under a QDRO, but his or her 58-year-old former spouse (and participant) usually would have to pay the penalty on a distribution. This provision in the law can be very upsetting to participants who feel like they are being treated unfairly. Remember, however, that although plan administrators can explain when the 10% penalty applies, they should never take sides in a squabble about which party should bear the tax consequences of a distribution. The plan administrator's job is to administer the plan according to its terms and to report distributions as required by law, regardless of whether those terms or reporting requirements seem fair to the participant or alternate payee.

Although plan administrators should not advise participants, potential alternate payees or their attorneys about the best way to structure a QDRO for tax purposes, plan administrators should be prepared to provide information about how various distributions are reported to the IRS. Like payments to participants, distributions to former spouse alternate payees are reported on Form 1099-R. For distributions to former spouses, the Form 1099-R should include the name and Social Security number of the former spouse, not the participant.[90]

Summary

In summary, federal law specifies when a plan administrator may treat a court order as a QDRO and assign benefits from a plan participant to an alternate payee. Plan administrators need to be familiar with both the requirements for QDROs and their own duties with respect to honoring QDROs. As discussed in the next two chapters, plan administrators can fulfill their legal obligations concerning QDROs more effectively through good communication and an organized system for managing QDROs.

Endnotes

1. IRC §414(p)(6)(B).
2. IRC §414(p)(6)(A)(i).
3. *Id.*
4. IRC §414(p)(6)(A)(ii).
5. See Gucciardi and Knox, *Pension Distribution Answer Book: Special Supplement—Forms & Worksheets*, 3-6 (generally 30 days is reasonable). See also Edmond and Landsman, "Do You or Don't You? The Nitty-Gritty on Domestic Relations Orders," 17 *Benefits & Compensation*, 48, 49 (1995) (one year is reasonable); Churchill, "Qualified Domestic Relations Orders: Traps for the Unwary," 1 *Journal of Pension Benefits*, 9, 12 (1994) (reasonable often means 18 months).
6. Report of American Bar Association's Section on Taxation, reprinted in *Highlights & Documents*, 3439, 3444 (March 3, 1995).
7. *Id.* at 3445.
8. IRC §414(p)(7)(A).
9. *Id.*
10. IRC §414(p)(7)(B).
11. IRC §414(p)(7)(E).
12. IRC §414(p)(7)(C).
13. IRC §414(p)(6)(B).
14. *CCH Compliance Guide for Plan Administrators*, 52 (April 8, 1994).
15. McCarthy, *Financial Planning for a Secure Retirement*, 25 (1996).
16. ERISA §206(D)(3)(J).
17. ERISA §105(a).
18. ERISA §105(b).
19. ERISA §206(d)(3)(J).
20. For a more detailed discussion of the argument that a potential alternate payee is entitled to information from the plan administrator, see Perdue, "QDROs and Qualified Plan Rules Pose Problems for Fiduciaries and Participants," 3 *Journal of Taxation of Employee Benefits*, 71, 72-73 (1995).
21. See *Hernandez v. Southern Nev. Culinary & Bartenders Pension Trust*, 662 F.2d 617, 621 (9th Cir. 1981) (widow of fully vested participant was not entitled to account information as a "beneficiary" under ERISA when the participant was not eligible for retirement benefits at the time of his death).
22. 25 F.3d 280 (5th Cir. 1994).
23. *Id.* at 281.
24. *Id.*
25. *Id.*
26. *Id.*
27. *Id.* at 280.
28. *Id.* at 281.
29. *Id.* at 282.
30. *Id.*
31. *Id.* at 283.
32. *Id.* at 282-83.
33. *Id.* at 282.
34. *Id.*

35. *Id.*

36. See Beam and Tacchino, "Employee Benefit Planning," 67 *Journal of the American Society of CLU & ChFC,* 8 (1993).

37. S. Rep't No. 99-313, 99th Cong., 2d Sess. 1105.

38. IRC §401(a)(11).

39. *Hopkins v. AT&T Global Information Solutions,* 105 F.3d 153, 20 EBC 2418 (4th Cir. 1997).

40. IRC §414(p)(7).

41. Gross, "How to Ensure That a DRO Qualifies Under the Detailed Tax and ERISA Requirements," 81 *Journal of Taxation,* 346, 348 (1994); "Established Procedures, Form Letters Keys to Successful QDRO Administration," *CCH Compliance Guide for Plan Administrators,* 214 (February 10, 1995).

42. "Established Procedures, Form Letters Keys to Successful QDRO Administration," *CCH Compliance Guide for Plan Administrators,* 214, 215 (February 10, 1995).

43. *Id.*

44. *Schoonmaker v. Employee Savings Plan of Amoco, Inc.*, 987 F.2d 410, 413 (7th Cir. 1993).

45. *Id.* at 410.

46. *Id.* at 413.

47. *Id.* at 412.

48. *Id.*

49. *Id.*

50. *Id.* at 414.

51. *Id.*

52. IRC §414(p)(6)(A)(ii).

53. See Zimmerman, "Taxing Retirement Distributions at Divorce in the Absence of a Qualified Domestic Relations Order," 73 *Taxes,* 326 (1995).

54. IRC §402(a)(1).

55. IRC §402(a)(9).

56. 20 EBC (BNA) 1513 (10th Cir. 1996).

57. *Id.* at 1514.

58. *Id.*

59. *Id.* at 1515.

60. *Id.*

61. *Id.*

62. *Id.*

63. *Id.* at 1523-24.

64. *Id.* at 1523.

65. *Id.*

66. *Id.*

67. *Id.*

68. 100 T.C. 521 (1993).

69. *Id.* at 522.

70. *Id.* at 522-23.

71. *Id.* at 523.

72. *Id.*

73. *Id.* at 523-24.

74. *Id.* at 531.

75. *Id.* at 526.
76. *Id.*
77. *Id.* at 529.
78. *Burton vs. Commissioner* T.C. Memo 1997-20.
79. IRC §4981A.
80. HR Rep. No. 526, 99th Cong., 2d Sess., pt. 2, at 27 (1986).
81. IRS Notice 89-25, Q&A-3.
82. *Id.*
83. *Id.*
84. IRC §402(e)(1)(B).
85. IRC §3405(c).
86. IRC §402(e)(1)(A) and §402(d)(4)(J).
87. Temp. Treas. Reg. 1.402(c)-2T, Q&A-10(b) (1992).
88. IRC §72(t).
89. IRC §72(t)(2)(c).
90. IRC §402(e)(1)(A).

Approaches to Communication

PLAN ADMINISTRATORS WHO DO NOT FOLLOW THE QDRO rules may face serious and expensive legal consequences even if they meant to follow them and made a mistake. Mistakes can result in improper distributions, which could lead to plan disqualification.[1] Plan administrators who fail to follow a valid order could be sued by alternate payees or participants who may have been harmed by a plan administrator's decisions.

With those concerns hanging over their heads, plan administrators may not give much priority to QDRO communication issues; however, a well-designed communication system can create a paper trail that a plan administrator can use to defend itself if litigation arises from a QDRO issue. That's why plan administrators should view the communication process as an opportunity to detail and defend their decisions made about court orders submitted for approval as QDROs.

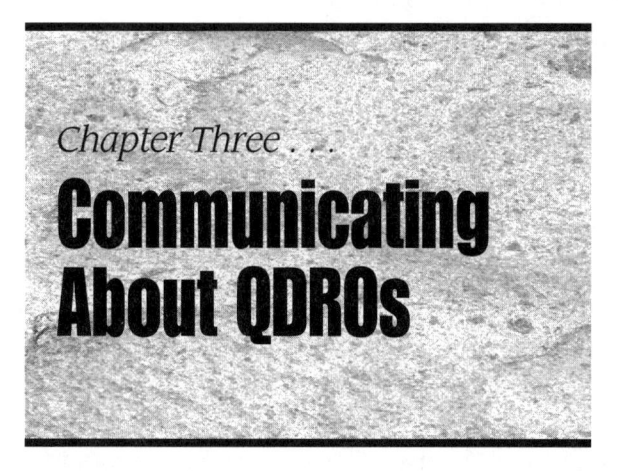

Chapter Three...
Communicating About QDROs

Minimum Communication

Some plan administrators have never given much thought to their QDRO communication strategies, or lack thereof. Plan administrators that do not handle many QDROs usually approach them on a case-by-case basis. They have not seen a need to develop streamlined QDRO communications because they have not had the experience of confronting the same situations or problems over and over again.

In this era of downsizing, rightsizing and reengineering, many plan administrators are learning to do more work with fewer people. At the same time, they have to keep up with a never-ending parade of new federal laws and regulatory developments affecting employee benefit plans. Given this environment, it's easy to understand why some plan administrators limit their communication about QDROs to the barest minimum required by law.

More Efficient Communication

Other plan administrators take a different approach than those who provide minimal communication—they go above and beyond what the law requires. Their efforts often save legal fees for both the participant and the alternate payee, either or both of whom may view the plan administrator as one more stumbling block in their divorce proceedings. When plan administrators adopt effective QDRO communication strategies, divorce lawyers don't have to spend as much time studying the terms of the plan and revising multiple drafts of defective orders.

Most plan administrators do not adopt effective QDRO communication techniques for altruistic reasons. They do it because they know their efforts will help reduce the amount of time and money *they* spend handling QDROs and related problems. One corporation estimated that it saved $200,000 a year by developing a sample package of information and a model QDRO for attorneys to use.[2] Plan administrators with good communication strategies probably decrease the likelihood that they will be sued by either a disgruntled participant or an alternate payee for mishandling a QDRO, although that theory would be difficult, if not impossible, to prove.

Private pension plans aren't the only ones providing more information than the law requires. In 1996, the Pension Benefit Guaranty Corporation (PBGC) released a booklet about its QDRO procedures.[3] The booklet includes sample forms for both defined benefit and defined contribution plans. Divorce attorneys and their clients should find this book quite helpful if they are working with plans handled by the PBGC. Former Labor Secretary Robert Reich recognized the importance of the booklet with these comments: "Husbands, wives, dependents, lawyers, and court officials rely on us [the PBGC] to provide answers about how to share one of the most important family resources. . . ."[4]

Congress recognized that divorce attorneys need some help in drafting orders. President Clinton signed the Small Business Job Protection Act in August of 1996, which included a little-noticed reference to QDROs.[5] It required the Secretary of the Treasury to develop sample language for inclusion in a form for a QDRO that meets the requirements of Code Section 414(p)(1)(A) and ERISA Section 206(d)(3)(B)(i).[6] This language is supposed to focus attention on the need to consider the treatment of any lump-sum payment, qualified joint and survivor annuity, or qualified preretirement survivor annuity.[7] The law required the Secretary of the Treasury to develop this language no later than January 1, 1997, and the Secretary was required to publicize it.[8]

In response to this law, the IRS issued Notice 97-11 in December 1996. The appendix to the notice includes sample QDRO language. This notice is discussed on pages 3 and 4 in Chapter One, although it doesn't tell plan administrators much they didn't already know. The text of the notice is reprinted on pages 105-121 in the appendix of this book.

Eventually, divorce attorneys may start using the sample PBGC language or language from Notice 97-11. This language may make communication efforts easier for some plan administrators. But depending on how the sample language works with the provisions of various plans, plan administrators may find that the government's sample language is more hindrance than help. Those plan administrators will then have the burden of educating attorneys about why the government's sample language won't work for their plan.

As divorce attorneys become more familiar with QDROs, and as spouses develop a better awareness of what pension benefits can be worth, plan administrators can expect to process more and more QDROs. That's why plan administrators should seriously consider their approach to communicating about QDROs. They should make an informed decision about whether they will meet the minimum communication standards required by law or whether they will take the time and effort to develop a more comprehensive communication technique that will save time and money in the long run. In other words, "How much of a divorce attorney's work do they want to do?"[9] The answer may be that the plan administrator prefers to do the attorney's work upfront rather than deal with the mistakes later.

Communication Required by Law

As discussed in Chapter One, federal law requires plan administrators to communicate certain information about QDROs. When an order is received, the plan administrator must notify the participant and each alternate payee that the order has been received.[10] At the same time, the plan administrator must advise the plan participant and the alternate payee of the plan's procedures for determining whether an order is a QDRO.[11] Then, within a reasonable period of time, the plan administrator must determine whether the order is a QDRO and notify the participant and alternate payee of that determination.[12]

Little Communication Required

The law does not require plan administrators to assist participants, alternate payees or their respective attorneys in preparing original or amended QDROs. If the plan administrator refuses to treat an order as a QDRO, the plan administrator has no legal duty to assist the attorney who prepared the order in correcting the deficiencies. Instead, the plan administrator can merely communicate that the order is not a QDRO. When plan administrators simply tell attorneys that an order is not a QDRO, the attorneys are on their own to find the magic language for an amended order.

When an attorney revises and resubmits an order, sometimes several times, participants and alternate payees can expect their legal fees to increase. Not surprisingly, these participants and alternate payees can wind up being very unhappy with the plan administrator because the plan administrator seems to be the cause of higher legal fees. Better communication about the problems with an order should reduce the parties' legal fees, spare the plan administrator the wrath of some unhappy people and cut down on the plan administrator's time spent in reviewing multiple defective orders.

Keeping Everyone in the Loop

Plan administrators often correspond directly with one or both attorneys representing the parties in a divorce. When both parties are represented by attorneys, plan administrators need to be careful about writing to one of the lawyers without sending copies of their letters to the other attorney. When plan administrators communicate only with one lawyer, they may leave the other party's attorney with the impression that information is being hidden. The potential alternate payee may already be suspicious of the plan administrator, particularly if the plan administrator is closely affiliated with the participant's employer.

When communicating with divorce attorneys, plan administrators need to remember that the attorney's time in reviewing every letter or answering every phone call will probably be billed to the plan participant or spouse. Few plan administrators needlessly send out information about QDROs, but participants and their spouses may be irked about paying the legal expenses associated with a QDRO. They know that it doesn't take that much attorney time to divide a bank account, and they often don't understand why dividing a pension plan is so complicated and time-consuming. That's one reason parties to a divorce sometimes view the plan administrator as wearing the black hat and needlessly giving the runaround to the divorcing couple or their attorneys.

Sometimes participants and alternate payees try to reduce their legal fees by communicating directly with the plan administrator. This situation can be extremely frustrating for plan administrators when the participant or spouse does not understand the plan administrator's directions or position. Unfortunately, some people think their tales of woe are more important than the legal requirements of a QDRO. Plan administrators may get letters from the participant's spouse accusing the participant of adultery or domestic violence. These people do not understand that the plan administrator does not need or want to know the gory details about the divorce—the plan administrator just wants to follow the QDRO rules.

Sometimes the participant or spouse does not pass along information to the attorneys, and the plan administrator winds up explaining the process more than once. When participants or spouses ask for information without giving the plan administrator the names of the attorneys, the plan administrator should emphasize how important it is for the attorneys to get the relevant information as soon as possible.

Communication about QDROs can be especially troublesome for attorneys representing the plan administrator. Participants and alternate payees may call or write the plan's attorney in an effort to save money on their own attorney fees. Attorneys generally have an ethical duty not to communicate directly with a party they know to be represented by an attorney. Sometimes plan attorneys and administrators have to be assertive about keeping all of the lawyers in the communication loop.

Parties Without Lawyers

Sometimes plan participants or alternate payees want to draft their own QDROs, particularly if they have not been represented by an attorney during their divorce. When plan administrators provide clear information and sample orders, some plan participants and alternate payees can successfully draft their own QDROs without an attorney. In fact, people who want to draft their own orders may be more willing to follow a plan administrator's instructions than a high-powered divorce attorney who thinks he or she has already drafted the world's best one-size-fits-all QDRO. Counsel for plan administrators need to be extremely careful to avoid the appearance of giving legal advice about a QDRO to either party, and they need to be particularly careful when the plan participant or alternate payee is working on a do-it-yourself QDRO.

Samples

The sample letters on the following pages can be used by plan administrators to communicate information about QDROs. Each sample letter is addressed to the plan participant, with a copy to the former spouse. In some cases, of course, the correspondence will be addressed to the former spouse with a copy going to the plan participant. In either case, the plan administrator should be sure that both parties get copies of the same information. Naturally, the letters need to be modified if they are directed to attorneys, or otherwise tweaked to fit individual plans and circumstances.

> **NOTE:** The following letter acknowledges receipt of an order and describes the plan's procedures for determining if the order is a QDRO.

Mr. John Doe
1234 Main Street
Anywhere, ST 00000

Re: Retirement Account of John Doe
   Account number: 55987

Dear Mr. Doe:

Thank you for sending us a copy of your divorce decree dated June 15, 1997. We received it on July 1, 1997.

Federal law requires us as a pension plan administrator to determine whether this order is a qualified domestic relations order (QDRO) under Section 414(p) of the Internal Revenue Code. I will send your divorce decree to our attorney who will review it and determine whether we can honor the order and assign benefits to your former wife, Mary Doe. For your information, I have enclosed a copy of the checklist our attorney will use to make that determination. **[NOTE: A sample checklist appears later in this chapter.]** You may recall that we previously sent you a package of information describing our QDRO procedures in more detail.

You can expect to receive a letter within the next 45 days advising you of our determination. If you have any questions about your rights to pension benefits under the order or about the QDRO rules, please consult your own attorney.

Very truly yours,

Jane Smith, CEBS
Benefits Administrator

cc: Mary Doe

NOTE: The following letter notifies the plan participant and alternate payee that the plan administrator has approved an order as a QDRO.

Mr. John Doe
1234 Main Street
Anywhere, ST 00000

Re: Retirement Account of John Doe
      Account number: 55987

Dear Mr. Doe:

The purpose of this letter is to notify you that our attorney has determined that your divorce decree is a qualified domestic relations order (QDRO) under Section 414(p) of the Internal Revenue Code. As required by the order, we will assign certain benefits to your former wife, Mary Doe. [NOTE: It may be helpful for the plan administrator to repeat the terms of the assignment in this letter. If the plan administrator has misunderstood the requirements of the order or if the order does not reflect the intentions of the parties, repeating the terms of the assignment in a letter should prompt the participant or alternate payee to correct the problem.]

Please notify us immediately if the order is amended or modified. Both of you should notify us if you have a change of address so that you will continue to receive information about your benefits.

Very truly yours,

Jane Smith, CEBS
Benefits Administrator

cc: Mary Doe

NOTE: This letter may be expanded as a transmittal letter for any additional forms the plan administrator needs to complete the assignment. For example, the letter could send each party beneficiary designation forms.

> **NOTE:** The following letter advises the plan participant that an order is not a QDRO. This letter does not offer assistance in correcting the order's problems.

Mr. John Doe
1234 Main Street
Anywhere, ST 00000

Re: Retirement Account of John Doe
    Account number: 55987

Dear Mr. Doe:

I regret to advise you that our attorney has determined that your divorce decree is not a qualified domestic relations order (QDRO) because it does not contain all of the information required by Section 414(p) of the Internal Revenue Code.

Enclosed is a copy of the checklist used to determine the status of the order. [NOTE: A sample checklist appears later in this chapter.] You should consult your own attorney to discuss the possibility of obtaining an amended order. If an amended order is entered by the court, please send a copy of it to me so that I can forward it to our attorney.

Very truly yours,

Jane Smith, CEBS
Benefits Administrator

cc: Mary Doe

Communicating About QDROs

> **NOTE:** The following letter advises the plan participant that an order is not a QDRO, but this letter offers more assistance in correcting the deficiencies.

Mr. John Doe
1234 Main Street
Anywhere, ST 00000

Re: Retirement Account of John Doe
Account number: 55987

Dear Mr. Doe:

I regret to advise you that our attorney has determined that your divorce decree is not a qualified domestic relations order (QDRO) because it does not contain all of the information required by Section 414(p) of the Internal Revenue Code.

As you will see from the enclosed checklist, the order does not specify the plans to which it applies. [NOTE: A sample checklist appears later in this chapter.] Our records indicate that you have participated in three different pension plans during your employment with the parent company and its subsidiaries. Enclosed is some additional information about those plans and the benefits to which you may be entitled due to your participation. [NOTE: The plan administrator may prefer to include benefit information either in the text of the letter or in a separate attachment. If the participant had not previously authorized the plan administrator to release benefit information to the former spouse, the plan administrator should avoid disclosing this information to the former spouse.] I suggest that you discuss this information with your attorney and consider the possibility of obtaining an amended order to correct this problem.

For your attorney's convenience, I have enclosed a sample QDRO. [NOTE: A sample QDRO appears later in this chapter.] If your attorney needs additional information about drafting an amended order, he or she may contact Sally Brown in our Legal Department at the address on this letterhead. We look forward to working with you and your attorney to resolve this matter.

Very truly yours,

Jane Smith, CEBS
Benefits Administrator

cc: Mary Doe

Optional Communication

As discussed earlier, plan administrators can satisfy their legal duty to communicate about QDROs with some relatively brief and simple letters. Nevertheless, in an effort to provide greater assistance to plan participants and their spouses and in an attempt to reduce administrative problems, some plan administrators prefer to provide more information about QDROs than the law requires. Of course, this information is most helpful if it is received before a final domestic relations order is entered by a court. Unfortunately, plan administrators often are not aware of a participant's divorce until it is already final.

Before an Order Is Drafted

Plan administrators who have an opportunity to work with a couple and their attorneys prior to entry of a final order can help ensure that the final order can be treated as a QDRO. When plan administrators reject orders as QDROs, they may feel the wrath of plan participants, their former spouses and their attorneys. By communicating with the parties before entry of a final order, plan administrators reduce the amount of time they spend reviewing defective orders and explaining the defects to the attorneys. A well-designed QDRO communication system should therefore reduce the plan's time and expenses for handling QDROs. As one commentator has observed: "Although plan administrators probably are not happy that plans may not charge specific participants or alternate payees for the cost of determining the qualified status of an order or for administering the order, it is still in their best interest to work with the participant's and alternate payee's advisors to obtain a DRO that is understandable and qualified."[13]

Working With Attorneys

Most employees do not understand their pension plans.[14] Moreover, many divorce lawyers do not have a background in employee benefits.[15] Domestic relations attorneys may not know the difference between a defined contribution plan and a defined benefit plan, and few of their clients know that either. Acronyms like ERISA and ESOP that roll off the tongues of plan administrators may sound like a foreign language to a domestic relations lawyer. Plan administrators and ERISA attorneys should not be snobbish about their expertise. After all, few ERISA attorneys could handle a complicated divorce or child custody case. Benefits professionals who are not attorneys probably know more about ERISA than the average divorce lawyer. Divorce lawyers don't need to know as much about ERISA as benefits professionals or ERISA attorneys—they simply need to know enough about the QDRO rules to represent the best interest of their clients.

Once a domestic relations attorney has successfully drafted a QDRO that has been honored by one plan administrator, the attorney may be in for a rude awakening when a similar order is rejected by another plan administrator. As one author has observed: "Even if an attorney is proficient at drafting QDROs, dealing with plan sponsors and administrators can quite often pose a more serious problem."[16] Some divorce attorneys think they can use a one-size-fits-all order, particularly if they have spent a lot of time drafting a long order with a lot of boilerplate and references to ERISA and the Code. Plan administrators for defined benefit plans often receive orders designed for defined contribution plans, and vice versa. When their clients don't know the legal name of the plans in which they participate or even what kinds of plans their employer sponsors, it's unreasonable to expect divorce attorneys to produce a flawless QDRO without some assistance. Clearly, an attorney attempting to draft a QDRO is at a distinct disadvantage unless the plan administrator willingly provides information.

When communicating with divorcing couples and their attorneys, plan administrators should attempt to use simple, clear language. Although using simple language to describe some aspects of pension plans is not an easy task, plan administrators should be able to develop procedures, forms and communication materials that can be understood by someone with no prior experience with their plan or any other pension plan. Plain language isn't patronizing, and other people probably wouldn't realize how difficult it is to convert employee benefit jargon into plain language.

A good communication system can help prevent attorneys from developing an adversarial relationship with plan administrators. When designing a QDRO communication system, plan administrators should remember the perspectives of the divorcing couple and their attorneys. Attorneys for potential alternate payees may question plan administrators' motives and may assume that plan administrators automatically side with participants during divorce. Although that assumption may be valid in some cases, the perception that plan administrators side with participants is probably due in part to the fact that many plan administrators have some close connection to the participant's employer or even to the participant. Additionally, plan administrators have a fiduciary duty to the participant, a duty not owed to the spouse until the spouse's rights as an alternate payee are established by a QDRO. Plan administrators who provide clear information to both sides are less likely to be treated as adversaries and potential defendants.

A divorce attorney's first contact with a plan administrator may be a request for information about the value of the plan participant's benefits. Often they want to know if the participant or spouse is eligible for an immediate distribution. Sometimes attorneys will ask for a copy of the plan document, although reading it and trying to decipher various plan provisions is probably a waste of time for the attorney. A summary plan description (SPD) or some other general explanation of the plan will usually be more helpful to a divorce attorney than the plan document itself.

Sample Packet

Often, after handling a number of divorce situations, plan administrators can recognize the questions most frequently asked by attorneys and their clients. These issues can be addressed in a letter or memo that includes basic information about the QDRO rules, the plan and the plan's procedures for processing QDROs. The letter or memo may be included in a packet of divorce information with all of the forms required to complete an assignment. Depending on the size of the packet, it may be helpful to have the forms printed on different colors of paper to avoid confusion. Plans may also choose to produce a booklet like that of the PBGC. Technological improvements in word processing, printing, copying and binding, even within the last ten years, have made it easier for plan administrators to produce this kind of information.

The following pages illustrate a sample QDRO communication system, one that provides more information than required by law.

NOTE: The following letter is for the spouse of a plan participant, but it can be edited to send to the plan participant or to an attorney. Sample memos to plan participants and attorneys follow this letter.

Mrs. Jane Doe
1234 Main Street
Anywhere, ST 00000

Re: Retirement Account of John Doe
      Account number 55987

Dear Mrs. Doe:

Thank you for letting us know that you and John Doe are in the process of getting a divorce and that you are making a claim to part of his retirement account. Enclosed is a memo that answers the questions most frequently asked by plan participants and their spouses about the effect of divorce on pension benefits. I'm also sending a copy of this information to Mr. Doe.

According to federal law, the plan cannot assign any of Mr. Doe's retirement benefits to you without a qualified domestic relations order (QDRO). Enclosed is an important package of information for you to give to your attorney that briefly describes how to prepare a QDRO. If Mr. Doe is represented by an attorney, his attorney should also have a copy of this information.

You have requested information about the value of Mr. Doe's retirement benefits. We cannot release that information without Mr. Doe's written consent or a subpoena. The enclosed package includes a consent form for Mr. Doe's signature. Please return it to me as soon as possible so I can send you the information you need.

If I can be of additional assistance, please feel free to contact me. If your attorney needs help in drafting a QDRO to meet our requirements, questions can be sent to Sally Brown in our Legal Department at the address on this letterhead.

Very truly yours,

Jane Smith, CEBS
Benefits Administrator

cc: John Doe

NOTE: The following memo answers some questions frequently asked by plan participants and their spouses. It does not discuss the QDRO rules in detail because those rules are discussed in a separate memo to attorneys following this one.

TO: Plan participants and their spouses

RE: Divorce

DATE: Revised October 31, 1997

Plan participants and their spouses often have the following questions about the effect of divorce on their retirement benefits:

1. **I earned my retirement benefits. Doesn't that mean they belong to me after divorce?**

Not necessarily. Under state law, a judge may award all or part of your benefits to your former spouse. Your attorney needs to consider your retirement benefits when drafting the divorce decree or property settlement agreement. If the plan participant will retain all rights to these retirement benefits, the court order should specifically say so. *XYZ Corporation cannot advise you whether these retirement benefits should be divided or how they should be divided. You need to consult your own attorney for assistance with those questions.*

2. **We have been married for a number of years and I think I'm entitled to part of my spouse's retirement benefits. Why do I need a court order to get my fair share?**

Federal law prohibits the assignment of pension benefits to a former spouse without a special court order called a "qualified domestic relations order" (QDRO). A QDRO assigns benefits to an "alternate payee," usually the former spouse or children of the participant. The enclosed memo to attorneys gives instructions for drafting a QDRO. Please be sure to give this information to each attorney as soon as possible.

3. **My former spouse is behind on child support payments. Can I have his retirement benefits garnished or attached?**

No. The plan cannot pay retirement benefits to a former spouse or children without a QDRO described in the answer to Question 2. If a court enters a valid QDRO, the plan will honor it.

Frequently Asked Questions—Continued

4. Before our divorce, my former spouse began receiving a joint and survivor annuity, and I expected to continue receiving benefits after his death. If he remarries, will his new spouse get that benefit?

No. A survivor benefit is payable to the person who was the spouse at the time the benefit was set up.

5. Can you advise me about the best way to divide this account for tax purposes?

No. We cannot give you any legal or tax advice about how to divide this account. Once you and your attorneys agree on your objectives, however, we can work with your attorney to draft an order that will meet those objectives. If you have any questions about the tax consequences of this assignment, you should consult your accountant or attorney.

6. Can my spouse withdraw retirement benefits before I get a QDRO?

If your spouse is not yet receiving a benefit, a benefit cannot be established without your written consent. The participant may continue to direct investments in this account until we approve an order as a QDRO. Once you make a written claim to a portion of the account, we usually restrict distributions from the account until you either release your claim or your rights are determined by a valid QDRO.

We will also permit benefits to be established or distributions to be processed if we have no further contact with the parties or their attorneys within 12 months and if you do not renew your claim in writing during that time. While we are reviewing an order to determine if it is a QDRO, we will separately account for any amounts that appear to be payable to an alternate payee. If we then decide that the order is not a QDRO, we will permit the plan participant to exercise all rights over those amounts for which we separately accounted if you do not notify us in writing within three weeks after you receive notice of rejection of the order that you are trying to have it corrected.

If a plan participant is already receiving benefits, we will continue to pay those benefits until we are presented with a domestic relations order. At that time, we will separately account for the benefits that appear to be payable to a potential alternate payee. If we then decide the order is not a QDRO, and if you do not notify us in writing within three weeks after receiving notice that we have rejected the order that you are trying to have the defective order corrected, we will pay those benefits for which we separately accounted to the participant.

NOTE: The following memo and attachments are directed to divorce attorneys, many of whom are not familiar with the QDRO rules.

This memo includes important information about divorce and pension benefits from XYZ Corporation. To avoid frustration and delays, please read this memo carefully before you draft a divorce decree or property settlement agreement referring to XYZ Corporation's pension plans.

TO: Attorneys representing participants or spouses of participants of XYZ Corporation's pension plans

RE: Assigning pension benefits after divorce

DATE: Revised October 31, 1997

XYZ's Pension Plans

[NOTE: This section should provide the complete names of the pension plans sponsored by XYZ and some basic information about the plans, for example, whether they are defined benefit or defined contribution plans. In lieu of giving detailed information about the plans, this section can refer to other enclosures such as SPDs or brochures.]

Distributions and Benefit Payments

Plan provisions and the Internal Revenue Code may prohibit or limit a participant or spouse from receiving an immediate distribution (withdrawal) of all or part of the plan accumulations at the time of divorce. XYZ Corporation cannot honor a divorce decree that orders a participant or spouse to receive an immediate distribution unless the distribution is permitted by the plan. Please consult us if you need specific information about distribution rights.

Retirement benefits are not like checking or savings accounts because the plan may not permit a distribution for a long time. After we have been notified in writing that the spouse is asserting a claim, we will not process a distribution or set up a benefit without the spouse's consent even if the plan permits the participant to make a withdrawal.

We will also permit benefits to be established or distributions to be processed if we have no further contact with the parties or their attorneys within 12 months and if the spouse does not renew a claim in writing during that time.

While we are reviewing an order to determine if it is a QDRO, we will separately account for any amounts that appear to be payable to an alternate payee. If we then decide that the order is not a QDRO, we will permit the

Communicating About QDROs

Memo to Divorce Attorneys—Continued

plan participant to exercise all rights over those amounts for which we separately accounted if the potential alternate payee does not notify us in writing within three weeks after receiving notice of rejection of the order that the deficiencies in the order are going to be corrected.

If a plan participant is already receiving benefits, we will continue to pay those benefits until we are presented with a domestic relations order. At that time, we will separately account for the benefits that appear to be payable to a potential alternate payee. If we then decide the order is not a QDRO, and if the alternate payee does not notify us in writing within three weeks after receiving notice that we have rejected the order that the order is going to be corrected, we will pay those benefits for which we separately accounted to the participant.

Qualified Domestic Relations Orders (QDROs)

The Retirement Equity Act of 1984 created special rules for assigning pension benefits after divorce. Those rules are found in Section 414(p) of the Internal Revenue Code and in Section 206(d) of the Employee Retirement Income Security Act of 1974 (ERISA). Before we can assign benefits to a former spouse, we must receive a qualified domestic relations order (QDRO) that complies with Section 414(p). The requirements of Section 414(p) are listed on the attached QDRO checklist (**hot pink form**). We use this checklist to determine if orders are QDROs.

For your convenience, a sample QDRO is enclosed (**yellow pages**). If you prefer to draft your own order, be sure to include the language in Paragraph 4 of the sample. The sample form includes language to divide benefits in half. This is a common arrangement; however, a court will ultimately have to determine what portion, if any, will be assigned.

The simplest arrangement is for the divorce decree to award the participant all retirement benefits. The parties may have to trade assets to make this arrangement work. If the parties choose this alternative, no QDRO is required and XYZ Corporation does not need to be involved. The parties can also agree that the participant will pay some of the benefits to the former spouse if and when benefits are paid. Under this arrangement, we cannot issue separate checks to the former spouse, nor can we help enforce the order in the event the participant violates it.

When a retirement benefit is set up, actuarial assumptions and calculations are made. That's why established benefits cannot be changed after a divorce. For example, if a participant elects a joint and survivor annuity at retirement and names his wife as the survivor, she will receive a survivor

Memo to Divorce Attorneys—Continued

benefit at his death. Even if the participant remarries, he cannot substitute his second wife as the survivor for his joint and survivor benefit.

How Assignments Are Made

When our attorney determines that we can honor an order as a QDRO, we will process the assignment. After a separate account is set up for the spouse, new beneficiary designation forms should be completed by both parties.

Please allow at least 45 days for approval of a QDRO after submission of all appropriate forms. If the QDRO orders a distribution and if the plan permits a distribution, allow a minimum of ten working days after approval of the QDRO and receipt of the other required forms for processing the distribution.

Tax Consequences

We cannot give personal tax advice. You need to advise your client about the tax consequences of an assignment or refer your client to a tax specialist.

Beneficiary Designations

As long as the parties are legally married, the spouse's signature is required before a participant may change his or her beneficiary. This requirement may be waived if a court has entered an order of legal separation.

Lapse of Time

Sometimes a spouse claims part of a retirement account benefit while a divorce is pending, but then we never receive any more information. Sometimes this is because the parties have reconciled and sometimes it is because the participant has retained all rights to the benefits. After 12 months from a notice of a claim by a spouse, we may permit the participant to exercise all rights unless the spouse re-asserts a claim in writing.

Additional Information

We will not release participant account information without a subpoena or the participant's notarized consent. A consent form is attached for your convenience **(green form)**. If a subpoena is issued, please direct it to the attention of our legal department.

If you need additional assistance, please contact our legal assistant, Sally Brown, at (000) 000-0000. Our fax number is (000) 000-0000. When you give us complete information about the parties' objectives, we can serve you better.

Please allow at least two weeks for a response.

[**NOTE:** Printed on Hot Pink Paper]

XYZ Corporation
Checklist for Qualified Domestic Relations Orders
Under Section 414(p) of the Internal Revenue Code

Participant Name: _____

Account No.: _____

Yes No

☐ ☐ 1. Is the order a domestic relations order?
An order is a *domestic relations order* if it is a judgment, decree, order, or approval of a property settlement which:
- Relates to the provision of child support, alimony payments, or marital property rights to a spouse (present or former), child, or other dependent of a plan participant; and
- Is made pursuant to a state domestic relations law, including a community property law.

A property settlement agreement which has not been approved by a court is not a domestic relations order.

☐ ☐ 2. Does the order contain the name and last known mailing address of the participant?

☐ ☐ 3. Does the order contain the name and last known mailing address of each alternate payee covered by the order?

☐ ☐ 4. Does the order create or recognize the rights of one or more alternate payee(s) (other than the participant) to receive all or part of the participant's plan benefits?
Alternate payee means any spouse, former spouse, child, or other dependent.

☐ ☐ 5. Does the order specify the amount or percentage of the participant's benefits to be paid by the plan to each alternate payee, or the manner in which such amount or percentage is to be determined?

QDRO Checklist—Continued

Yes No

☐ ☐ 6. Does the order specify the number of payments or the period to which such order applies?

☐ ☐ 7. Does the order contain the name of the plan(s) (XYZ Pension Plan) to which it applies?

☐ ☐ 8. Does the order provide benefits at a time or in a form that is available under the plan document?

☐ ☐ 9. Does the order only require the plan to provide benefits that do not exceed the participants' plan benefits?

☐ ☐ 10. Does the order refrain from affecting any benefits of a prior known QDRO?

Date Order Received: _____

Reviewed By: _____ **Date:** _____

Comments:
_____
_____
_____
_____
_____

[**NOTE:** Printed on Yellow Paper]

Qualified Domestic Relations Order

This sample QDRO incorporates all the requirements of Section 414(p) of the Internal Revenue Code and is an example of an order XYZ Corporation would treat as a QDRO. You may include the language in a separate order or in the divorce decree itself. We cannot give individual tax advice or advice about the marital property rights of either party.

1. Pursuant to Section 414(p) of the Internal Revenue Code, this qualified domestic relations order (Order) assigns a portion of the benefits in the XYZ Pension Plan (the Plan) from ___[participant's name]___ ("Participant") (account no. _____) to ___[spouse's name]___ ("Alternate Payee") in recognition of the existence of his/her marital rights in Participant's retirement account.

2. Participant in the Plan is ___[participant's name]___, Social Security no. _____, whose last known mailing address is _____.

3. Alternate Payee is ___[spouse's name]___, Social Security no. _____, whose last known mailing address is _____.

NOTE: Select *one* paragraph 4 from the choices below.

[Use the following paragraph if the participant is not already receiving retirement benefits from a defined contribution plan.]

4. XYZ Corporation is hereby ORDERED to assign a portion of the accumulations so that each party as of the date of the assignment has a retirement account of approximately the same value. The date of assignment is _____.

[Use the following paragraph if the participant is assigning a specific dollar amount to the spouse from a defined contribution plan.]

4. XYZ Corporation is hereby ORDERED to assign $_____ as of _____ (date) from Participant's account to an account for Alternate Payee.

[Use the following paragraph if the participant is already receiving benefits from a defined contribution or a defined benefit plan.]

4. XYZ Corporation is hereby ORDERED to make monthly payments equal to one-half of the amount payable to Participant directly to Alternate Payee. These direct payments to Alternate Payee shall be made beginning after the date of this Order and shall end at Participant's death.

QDROs: A Guide for Plan Administration

Sample QDRO—Continued

[Use the following paragraph if the participant is not already receiving retirement benefits from a defined benefit plan.]

4. XYZ Corporation is hereby ORDERED to assign ____% of Participant's present accrued benefit to Alternate Payee. Alternate Payee shall have the right to begin receiving benefit payments from the Plan on or after the date on which Participant attains or would have attained the earliest retirement age under the Plan. In determining the benefit, the present value of any employer subsidy for early retirement shall not be considered; however, Alternate Payee shall be entitled to any cost-of-living increases as a proportionate share of Alternate Payee's interest in the total benefit. Additionally, Alternate Payee shall be entitled to a proportionate share of any early retirement subsidy granted to Participant if Participant elects to retire prior to the normal retirement age.

    In the event Participant dies before Alternate Payee, Alternate Payee will be entitled to a joint and survivor annuity based on the accrued joint and survivor benefit on the date of death.

    If Participant dies before any retirement benefits are paid from the Plan, Alternate Payee shall receive a preretirement survivor annuity based on the percentage of the accrued preretirement survivor benefit on the date of divorce in proportion to the accrued preretirement survivor benefit on the date of death.

5. This qualified domestic relations order is not intended to require the Plan to provide any type or form of benefits or any option not otherwise provided by the Plan, nor shall this Order require the Plan to provide for increased benefits not required by the Plan. This Order does not require the Plan to provide benefits to Alternate Payee that are required to be paid to another alternate payee under another order previously determined to be a qualified domestic relations order.

6. All benefits payable under the Plan other than those payable to Alternate Payee shall be payable to Participant in such manner and form as s/he may elect in his/her sole and undivided discretion, subject only to Plan requirements.

7. Alternate Payee is ORDERED to report any retirement payments received on any and all appropriate income tax returns. XYZ Corporation is authorized to issue any and all appropriate Internal Revenue forms or reports to the Internal Revenue Service for any direct payments made to Alternate Payee.

8. While it is anticipated that XYZ Corporation will pay directly to Alternate Payee the benefit awarded to her/him, Participant is designated a constructive trustee to the extent s/he receives any retirement benefits under the Plan that are due to Alternate Payee but paid to Participant. Participant is ORDERED AND DECREED to pay the benefit defined above directly to Alternate Payee within three days after receipt by him/her.

[**NOTE:** Printed on Green Paper]

Consent Form

I hereby authorize XYZ Corporation to give information about my pension plan(s) to my attorney, _____,
and to_____ and his/her attorney.

                 Participant's Signature: _____
                 Name (printed): _____
                 Account No.: _____
                 Date: _____

STATE OF_____

COUNTY OF _____

Before me, the undersigned notary, on this day personally appeared _____, known to me, or proved to me on the basis of satisfactory evidence, to be the person whose name is subscribed to the foregoing instrument, and acknowledged to me that s/he executed the same for the purposes and consideration herein expressed.

GIVEN UNDER MY HAND AND SEAL OF OFFICE, this _____ day of _____, 19___.

                 _____
(Seal)   Notary Public in and for: _____
                 Name (print): _____
                 My commission expires: _____

Summary

In summary, plan administrators have a legal obligation to communicate certain information about QDROs to plan participants and alternate payees. Legally, plan administrators may be required to communicate very little information, but they can provide extra service by giving additional information to plan participants, their spouses and attorneys prior to the time the divorce is final. Regardless of the approach to communication, plan administrators can use form letters and memos to help ensure consistency and to promote efficient administration of QDROs.

Endnotes

1. Norquist, "Qualified Domestic Relations Orders: A Plan Administrator's Operational Perspective," 11 *Benefits Quarterly*, 76 (1995).
2. "Established Procedures, Form Letters Keys to Successful QDRO Administration," *CCH Compliance Guide for Plan Administrators*, 214 (February 10, 1995).
3. *Divorce Orders & PBGC*. Available from the PBGC QDRO Coordinator, P.O. Box 19153, Washington, D.C. 20036-0153; or from the PBGC's service center at (800) 400-PBGC; or from the PBGC's home page at http://www.pbgc.gov.
4. "PBGC Publishes Information Booklet on Submitting QDROs for Approval," 23 *BNA Pension & Benefits Reporter*, 2207 (1996).
5. PL 104-188, §1457, 110 Stat. 1755, 1818-19 (1996).
6. *Id.*
7. *Id.* at 1819.
8. *Id.*
9. "Established Procedures, Form Letters Keys to Successful QDRO Administration," *CCH Compliance Guide for Plan Administrators*, 214 (February 10, 1995).
10. IRC §414(p)(6)(A)(i).
11. *Id.*
12. IRC §414(p)(6)(A)(ii).
13. Gross, "How to Ensure That a DRO Qualifies Under the Detailed Tax and ERISA Requirements," 81 *The Journal of Taxation*, 346, 352 (1994).
14. McCarthy, *Financial Planning for a Secure Retirement*, 25 (1996).
15. Murtha, "Divorce Is Hard on Benefits Managers," 12 *Crain's New York Business*, 22 (1996).
16. Shulman, "Your Client's Entitlement to Pension Benefits: Understanding QDROs," 6 *American Journal of Family Law*, 197 (1992).

Introduction

To ensure compliance with the law and to reduce problems with administration, plan administrators need an efficient system for managing paperwork related to QDROs. To some extent, the design of an effective system for managing QDRO paperwork may depend on the size of the plan, the size of the plan administrator and on the plan administrator's recordkeeping system. Plan administrators that handle only a few QDROs annually may not see the need for an organized system. But regardless of whether a plan receives one QDRO or over 100 QDROs a year, plan administrators should consider how they can more efficiently handle the process.

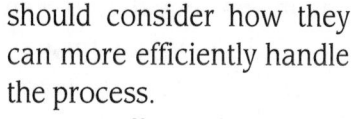

Chapter Four...
Managing QDROs

To effectively manage QDROs, plan administrators need to focus on three things. First, plan administrators must develop procedures for handling QDROs. Second, plan administrators should select and train the appropriate person or persons responsible for making decisions about QDROs. Finally, plan administrators need to simplify internal communication about QDROs. This chapter will discuss how plan administrators can meet these three objectives with an efficient QDRO management system.

Need for Management Procedures

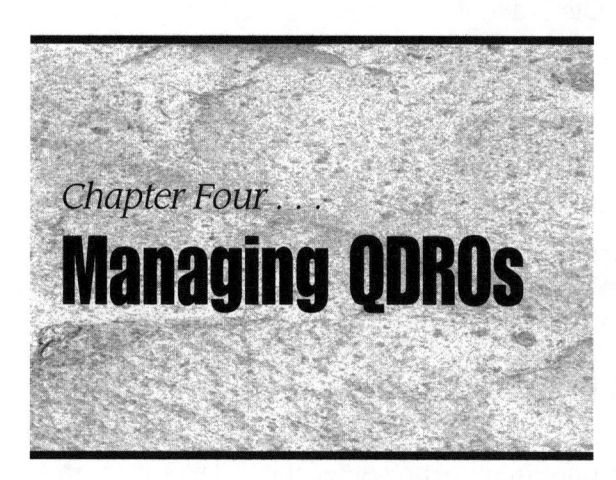

As discussed in previous chapters, plan administrators have a number of legal obligations with respect to QDROs, one of which is to establish procedures for determining whether an order is a QDRO.[1] By law, plan administrators must "promptly" notify any participant and alternate payee of the receipt of a domestic relations order.[2] Then the plan administrator has a "reasonable" amount of time to determine the status of the order.[3] There are no statutory guidelines defining *promptly* or *reasonable*, so plan administrators have some flexibility in creating their own timetables.

Plan administrators should not have to impose unreasonable demands on their legal counsel or other personnel to approve or reject orders, or to complete assignments and distributions ordered by QDROs. Nevertheless, when QDROs require immediate distributions, plan administrators can expect pressure from the parties and their lawyers to approve them. When orders are defective, they are generally easier to amend immediately after divorce rather than months later when the parties may have moved or lost contact with their attorneys. That is why prompt rejection of a defective order by a plan administrator may significantly affect the ability of the parties to present the plan administrator with an acceptable order.

If the plan administrator has an opportunity to communicate with the couple and their attorneys prior to entry of the final order, the timetable can be explained upfront so that everyone will know what to expect. As a practical matter, plan administrators may want to make processing QDROs a high priority to avoid hostility from participants, alternate payees and their lawyers. Nevertheless, plan administrators have no legal duty to jump through flaming hoops for an attorney who calls at 4:45 on a Friday afternoon asking for information to be used at a final divorce hearing first thing Monday morning.

Restricting Distributions

As previously discussed, plan administrators need to be especially careful about making distributions once they are presented with a DRO to approve as a QDRO. While the plan administrator is considering whether an order is a QDRO, the plan administrator must separately account for the amounts that would have been payable to the alternate payee if the order had been determined to be a QDRO.[4]

A plan administrator that determines an order is not a QDRO is faced with a dilemma about whether to permit the participant to receive a distribution if a participant's former spouse is still asserting a claim.[5] This is a common problem because defective orders are prevalent, despite the fact that QDROs have been in the law since 1984.[6] Statutory legislative history supports plan administrators that freeze benefits if one of the parties advises the plan administrator that an acceptable order is being sought;[7] however, plan administrators need more guidance on this issue.[8] Plan administrators that decide to restrict distributions or investment rights at any point in the QDRO process should be sure their practices conform to their written procedures.[9]

To avoid processing a distribution to a participant in violation of Section 414(p) or the plan's QDRO procedures, plan administrators need a system for warning their employees that important legal issues are not resolved. To prevent distributions that violate the terms of a QDRO or the plan's written procedures, plan administrators should be able to flag participants' records to indicate a divorce is pending or that an order is being evaluated to determine whether it is a QDRO.

During the next few years, more plan administrators will probably begin document imaging, a process that will ultimately replace many plan participants' paper records. Currently, however, most plan administrators have a combination of computer and paper records for participants. A warning that a divorce is pending should appear on both computerized records and paper files. If the plan maintains files about each participant, folders of divorcing participants should be clearly marked on the outside so correspondence about the divorce doesn't get overlooked. For example, the outside of the folder could be stamped "Important Divorce Information Inside Folder." A memorandum with the following warning could be stapled inside the folder: "This participant is in the process of a divorce. Do not release any information about retirement benefits without the written consent of the participant. Distributions should not be permitted without prior approval from legal counsel."

Organizing Paperwork

The person who ultimately makes the decision about whether an order is a QDRO should receive copies of all correspondence leading up to the QDRO. For example, if the plan administrator's attorney determines if an order is a QDRO, he or she needs to have easy access to correspondence, including memos about telephone conversations. The person who makes the final determination will therefore accumulate files about each divorce and will be in a better position to respond to questions from the couple or their attorneys. Copies of important information should also be placed in the participant's individual master folder if one is maintained by the plan administrator. Document imaging and increasingly sophisticated recordkeeping software should ultimately reduce paper shuffling as more people have electronic access to participant information at their fingertips.

If the plan processes a number of QDROs each year, the person responsible for deciding the status of orders may want to keep divorce files separate from other matters to improve access to information. Instead of file folders, three-ring binders with tab dividers make an efficient system for managing QDRO paperwork. Plan administrators that handle only a few QDROs annually may need only two notebooks, one for names beginning with A-L and another for names beginning with M-Z. Plan administrators that handle a lot of QDROs annually will obviously need more notebooks.

After a divorce is final and all issues relating to a QDRO have been resolved, the paperwork can be transferred into notebooks for "closed" divorces. Depending on the plan administrator's record retention program, these files can ultimately be microfilmed or sent offsite for storage. This system will undoubtedly sound like it's from the Stone Age as document imaging and similar technology becomes more prevalent.

Regardless of whether the plan administrator uses files or notebooks, the plan administrator should be able to identify the names and addresses of the parties and their lawyers without digging through the file. A cover sheet inserted after a divider tab in a notebook or attached to the inside of a file folder provides easy access to this information. Cover sheets can be completed by hand; however, they will be easier to update if they are kept as word processing documents. As the parties' addresses change or if they change attorneys, the cover sheet will be a quick reference for the plan administrator.

The following form is an example of a cover sheet about divorcing participants. Like the other forms in this book, it should be modified to meet the specific needs of the plan administrator. For example, some plan administrators may want a place for the name of the plan sponsor or for the participant's employer. Plan administrators may also want a place on the form to indicate which employee opened and closed the file.

NOTE: The following cover sheet is designed to provide quick access to information about each divorce file.

Date opened: _____

Participant's name: Account no.:

Participant's address:

   Phone:

Participant's attorney and address:

   Phone:

Spouse's name: Account no.:
                                                (if applicable)

Spouse's address:

   Phone:

Spouse's attorney and address:

   Phone:

Date closed: _____

Fees for QDROs

Even with a well-organized system for handling QDROs, administration is time-consuming and often involves numerous letters and long-distance calls. The author has heard many plan administrators observe that there seems to be an inverse relationship between the size of the benefit and the time and effort the plan administrator devotes to processing a QDRO. In other words, the smallest accounts or benefits seem to require more special handling than the larger accounts or benefits. While there is no empirical evidence to support this view, anecdotal evidence suggests that when divorcing couples have fewer assets to divide, the pension plan is more likely to be divided.

In divorce cases where there are few marital assets, often one party won't be represented by an attorney. That means the plan administrator may have to explain the QDRO rules to a nonattorney. When there are significant marital assets, however, the husband and wife generally each have an attorney. Attorneys who frequently represent clients with a lot of assets are probably more familiar with QDROs than attorneys who prefer to handle a large volume of "simple" divorces.

Individual Fees

Under ERISA, plan assets must be used for the exclusive benefit of participants and beneficiaries and for paying reasonable costs of plan administration.[10] Therefore, it's clear that plans can pay the costs of reviewing and processing QDROs as long as those costs are reasonable.[11] As plans began to confront the costs of QDRO administration, some began to charge individual participants for processing QDROs, rather than spreading the costs across all plan participants.

By 1991, when the first edition of this book was published, a number of plan administrators were either charging fees for processing QDROs to individual participants or seriously considering it. The Department of Labor had suggested that expenses directly related to a QDRO could be charged to a participant's account.[12] Some plans were charging flat fees of up to $300 for processing QDROs. Other plans based their fees on what the plan paid for actuarial and legal advice in processing each QDRO.

Rather than asking participants and alternate payees to send checks for processing QDROs, plan administrators for defined contribution plans that charged fees could deduct half the fee from the accumulations of each party.

Plan administrators for defined benefit plans, on the other hand, generally rejected this approach because they were uncertain how to subtract a fee from a defined benefit plan that was not yet being paid.

Department of Labor Position

In 1994, the Department of Labor (DOL) addressed QDRO fees in ERISA Advisory Opinion 94-32A. In that advisory opinion, the DOL concluded that a plan administrator could not charge individual fees for administering and processing QDROs. Only the parties to an ERISA advisory opinion may rely on it; however, this advisory opinion is instructive because it is the clearest statement by the DOL of its opinion. Plan administrators are likely to adhere to it even though technically they may not "rely" on it.

The DOL issued Advisory Opinion 94-32A in response to a request for an opinion by the VIZ Manufacturing Company about a profit-sharing plan. The company was considering a plan amendment that would charge individual participant accounts for the cost of determining whether an order was a QDRO and for administering it.

After reviewing ERISA and parallel provisions in the Code, the DOL decided the plan could not be amended to charge QDRO fees. The DOL noted that Section 206(d)(3) of ERISA gives an alternate payee the right to receive benefits payable because of a QDRO. Therefore, the DOL concluded that "a plan may not encumber the exercise of a right mandated by Title I of ERISA by imposing conditions on the exercise of a right that is not contemplated by the statute." Title I does not require or permit a plan to impose separate fees or costs related to determining the status of a domestic relations order or administering a QDRO "apart from the appropriate allocation of reasonable administrative expenses of the plan as a whole. . . ."

In conclusion, the DOL said:

Accordingly, it is the view of the Department that imposing a separate fee or cost on a participant or alternate payee (either directly or as a charge against a plan account) in connection with a determination of the status of a domestic relations order or administration of a QDRO would constitute an impermissible encumbrance on the exercise of the right of an alternate payee, under Title I of ERISA, to receive benefits under a QDRO. Additionally, in the Department's view, because Title I of ERISA imposes specific statutory duties on plan administrators regarding QDRO determinations and the administration of QDROs, reasonable administrative expenses thus incurred by the plan may not appropriately be allocated to the individual participants and beneficiaries affected by the QDRO.

In a footnote, the DOL pointed out that plan administrators must follow reasonable procedures in administering QDROs and "must assure that the plan pays only reasonable expenses of administering the plan, as required by Sections 403(c)(1) and 404(a)(1)(A) of ERISA." The DOL concluded: "In this regard, it is the view of the Department that plan fiduciaries must take appropriate steps to ensure that plan procedures are designed to be cost effective and to minimize expenses associated with the administration of domestic relations orders." Certainly the DOL's decision that plans cannot charge individual participants for processing QDROs is an incentive for plans to design cost-effective systems for managing them.

Selecting and Training Personnel

To promote efficiency and consistency in managing QDROs, the plan administrator should designate one person to be primarily responsible for making decisions and maintaining information about QDROs. If the plan administrator is large enough, some of this person's duties can be delegated to other staff. For example, even if an attorney routinely approves QDROs, a nonlawyer can supply information about the value of benefits under the plan and about plan features such as distribution rights. A legal assistant can field routine calls from attorneys, referring more difficult questions to the attorney as appropriate.

The person with responsibility for approving QDROs should train other staff about the plan's procedures and communications material. As a practical matter, a limited number of people should be assigned to give out information about divorces. Limiting the number of people providing information about QDROs will help ensure consistency in communication and procedures.

> **NOTE:** The following sample memo instructs employees of a plan administrator how to respond to routine inquiries about divorce.

TO: Benefit Supervisors

RE: XYZ Corporation's QDRO Procedures

DATE: Revised October 31, 1997

1. **When a divorce is already final**

XYZ Corporation may not learn of a participant's divorce until it is already final, at which time we may not be able to be of much assistance. No action needs to be taken if XYZ is notified of a divorce after the fact as long as the spouse has not asserted a claim. If a participant or former spouse notifies you that a former spouse is making a claim to retirement benefits after a divorce, take the following steps:

- Ask the person to send you a copy of the final divorce decree and/or property settlement agreement that mentions the XYZ Corporation's Pension Plan so that you can send it to the Legal Department for review.
- Advise the inquiring party that unless the final decree or property settlement agreement is a qualified domestic relations order (QDRO) that specifically awards a portion of the account to the former spouse, XYZ cannot make an assignment.
- Use the following response when the divorce decree does not mention the pension plan but when the former spouse is still asserting a claim to benefits:

    You have advised me that your divorce decree does not mention [your/your spouse's] retirement benefits from XYZ Corporation. XYZ Corporation cannot assign retirement benefits to a former spouse unless XYZ is presented with a valid qualified domestic relations order (QDRO). A QDRO is a special court order defined by Section 414(p) of the Internal Revenue Code. Please show this letter to your attorney, preferably the one who represented you during your divorce, so that you can decide whether to return to court to obtain an amended order. Your attorney should contact me for a package of information about XYZ's requirements for QDROs.

    Your decision about whether to obtain an amended order may depend on the value of the account. XYZ Corporation cannot release confidential account information without a subpoena or a plan par-

Managing QDROs

Sample Memo—Continued

ticipant's written notarized consent. Enclosed is a consent form for the plan participant's signature.

2. When a divorce is pending

Participants should receive the following information:
- Cover letter, including plan information.
- Memo for plan participants and their spouses.
- Memo to attorneys concerning divorce (multicolored packet).

Spouses (or attorneys for either party) should receive the following information:
- Cover letter without account information.
- Memo for participants and their spouses.
- Memo to attorneys concerning divorce (multicolored packet).
- Send copies of all correspondence concerning divorce to the Legal Department.
- If there are any unusual circumstances about this situation, immediately notify the Legal Department.
- When the spouse makes a written claim to part of the retirement account, put the Important Information stamp on the participant's master folder and add the distribution alert flag to the participant's RECORD screen.

3. Completing an assignment

- When you receive a divorce decree or property settlement agreement, send them to the Legal Department for review and take steps to separately account for what appears to be the alternate payee's share. If the order is approved as a QDRO, someone in the Legal Department will ask you to establish a separate account for the alternate payee.
- Set up the alternate payee's account like a new participant's account.
- Create a separate folder for the alternate payee's new account. The participant's and alternate payee's folders should cross reference each other in case additional information is needed at a later date.
- Remove the Important Information stamp from the participant's folder and the distribution alert flag from the participant's RECORD screen.
- After the assignment is complete, send a confirmation letter to the participant and alternate payee with beneficiary designation forms and any additional information they may have requested.
- Send a copy of your confirmation letter to the Legal Department.

Simplifying Internal Communication

As discussed in previous chapters, form letters and memos can improve communication between the plan administrator and outside contacts such as participants, their spouses and their attorneys. But in addition to communicating with these third parties, large plan administrators may have a number of different departments or personnel communicating internally as part of the QDRO process. Like external communication, internal communication can be streamlined and simplified.

The plan administrator needs to educate its staff about who will handle inquiries about divorce and QDROs. Otherwise, employees who routinely provide benefit information to participants could unknowingly overlook important details affecting QDROs. Initial letters about divorce from attorneys and plan participants may not be addressed to a specific person in the plan administrator's office or they may be addressed to the wrong person. Even subpoenas have a way of floating around from desk to desk if employees do not know where to send them. Inexperienced employees may not be able to "read between the lines" of a letter seeking information for a QDRO if the letter does not specifically mention divorce. Some plan administrators may find it helpful to instruct mail room personnel to route all correspondence from attorneys that is not addressed to a specific person at the plan administrator to the legal department, if the plan administrator has one. If the plan administrator does not have a legal department, letters from attorneys should routinely be routed to someone who can assess their urgency and involve outside legal counsel if appropriate. This is a helpful procedure for managing correspondence about legal issues even if the correspondence is not about QDROs.

Telephone conversations with plan participants, alternate payees or their lawyers should be documented in writing, either in a telephone memorandum, electronic mail (which can be printed) or in a letter confirming the conversation. Plan administrators that handle a large number of QDROs annually cannot possibly remember all the details of a particular case. Memos about telephone conversations are especially helpful to convey information to another employee of the plan administrator who will be affected by the conversation. Additionally, written documentation is helpful in the event the attorney or participant misunderstands instructions and accuses the plan administrator of making an error. Document imaging and recordkeeping software that permit this information to be shared by the plan administrator's employees will improve communications between everyone involved in this process.

NOTE: The following sample telephone memo may assist another person or department involved in processing QDROs.

CALL FROM: John Doe (Account No. 12345)

TELEPHONE NUMBER: (000) 000-0000

PERSON ANSWERING CALL: Jane Smith

DATE: August 7, 1997

John Doe called to say that he and his wife had agreed that he would take an immediate distribution from the plan and pay her half of it before their divorce is final. I told him that I would send him the appropriate forms and that his wife would have to sign a special release because she had previously made a claim to this account. I told him he could expect to receive the forms within two weeks and that the forms should be returned to the Benefits Department.

> **NOTE:** Instead of a telephone memo, plan administrators may prefer to document telephone conversations with a letter like the following sample.

Mr. John Doe
1234 Main Street
Anywhere, ST 00000

Re: John Doe
       Account Number 12345

Dear Mr. Doe:

Thank you for your telephone call of August 3 in which you advised me that you and your wife had agreed for you to receive an immediate distribution from your pension plan so that you can pay her half of the benefits before your divorce is final. As we discussed, enclosed are the forms and information you need to complete to request the distribution.

I am sending a copy of this letter to your wife along with the special release she will need to sign because she had previously made a claim to some of these benefits. [**NOTE:** A sample release of claim to retirement account is included in Chapter Two on page 33.]

Please return these forms at your earliest convenience to our Benefits Department. Your distribution will be processed approximately three weeks after we receive the completed forms. If you have any questions about the forms, please do not hesitate to contact me.

Very truly yours,

Jane Smith, CEBS
Benefits Administrator

When several employees or departments are involved in handling QDROs, plan administrators can improve and simplify internal communication with form memos or standard electronic mail messages. Memo forms can be kept in shared directories on a network for easy access. Carbonless forms or photocopies also work. Some examples follow.

NOTE: The following memo may be used when the plan administrator first receives notice of a pending divorce.

TO: Mary Roe
Benefits Supervisor

FROM: Sally Brown
Legal Assistant

RE: New Divorce
Participant name: _____
Account no.: _____

DATE: _____

We have been notified that this participant has a divorce pending, and the spouse has made a written claim to a portion of this retirement account. Please place the Distribution Alert flag on the participant's RECORD screen and the Important Information stamp on the participant's folder.

Please send the standard letter and divorce package to:

_____
_____
_____
_____

Remember to send a copy of your letter to the Legal Department. Thank you for your assistance.

NOTE: The following memo confirms that an order has been approved as a QDRO and gives instructions for making the assignment.

TO: Mary Roe
Benefits Supervisor

FROM: Sally Brown
Legal Assistant

RE: New Divorce
Participant name: _____
Account no.: _____

DATE: _____

The Legal Department has determined that the attached order is a QDRO. Please take the following action and send the Legal Department a copy of any final transmittal letters so we will know to close our file:

☐ 1. Please set up a separate account for _____ with _____% of the accumulations in _____'s account as of _____.

☐ 2. After receipt of the appropriate forms, please process a withdrawal for _____ of _____% of the accumulations in _____'s account as of _____.

☐ 3. Please begin sending benefit checks in the amount of $_____ to _____.

☐ 4. Other instructions: _____
_____
_____
_____

☐ This divorce has been completed, and the spouse was not awarded any interest in the participant's retirement benefits.

After you have taken the appropriate action, please remove the Distribution Alert flag from the participant's RECORD screen and the Important Information stamp from the participant's folder. Thank you.

Managing QDROs

Summary

In summary, plan administrators can better manage QDROs by developing efficient procedures, training the right personnel and simplifying internal communication. Plan administrators need to establish routines to avoid making improper distributions, and they need to organize QDRO paperwork to make it easily accessible. Handling QDROs can be extremely time-consuming for plan administrators, but an organized system can substantially reduce the administrative burden. Increased use of document imaging as well as more sophisticated recordkeeping software should make life easier in the future for plan administrators processing QDROs.

Endnotes

1. IRC §414(p)(6)(B).
2. IRC §414(p)(6)(A)(i).
3. IRC §414(p)(6)(A)(ii).
4. IRC §414(p)(7)(A).
5. See *id.*
6. Westbrook, "Update on Qualified Domestic Relations Orders, 25 *The Pension Actuary*, 6, 8 (1995).
7. S. Rep. 313, 99th Cong. 2d Sess. 1105 (1986).
8. Report of the American Bar Association's Section on Taxation, reprinted in *Highlights & Documents*, 3439, 3446 (March 3, 1995).
9. *Schoonmaker v. Employee Savings Plan of Amoco Corp.*, 987 F.2d 410 (7th Cir. 1993).
10. ERISA §404(a)(1).
11. See *id.*
12. See "QDRO Determination Expenses May Be Charged to Certain Plans," 17 *Tax Management Compliance Journal*, 249 (1989).

These are the most current laws at the time of publishing. Please consult an attorney for any changes or updates.

Internal Revenue Code
Section 414(p)
26 U.S.C. §414(p)

(p) **Qualified Domestic Relations Order Defined.**—For purposes of this subsection and Section 401(a)(13)—

(1) **In general.**—

(A) Qualified domestic relations order.—The term "qualified domestic relations order" means a domestic relations order—

(i) which creates or recognizes the existence of an alternate payee's right to, or assigns to an alternate payee the right to, receive all or a portion of the benefits payable with respect to a participant under a plan, and

(ii) with respect to which the requirements of paragraphs (2) and (3) are met.

(B) Domestic relations order.—The term "domestic relations order" means any judgment, decree, or order (including approval of a property settlement agreement) which—

(i) relates to the provision of child support, alimony payments, or marital property rights to a spouse, former spouse, child, or other dependent of a participant, and

(ii) is made pursuant to a State domestic relations law (including a community property law).

(2) **Order must clearly specify certain facts.**—A domestic relations order meets the requirements of this paragraph only if such order clearly specifies—

(A) the name and the last known mailing address (if any) of the participant and the name and mailing address of each alternate payee covered by the order,

(B) the amount or percentage of the participant's benefits to be paid by the plan to each such alternate payee, or the manner in which such amount or percentage is to be determined,

(C) the number of payments or period to which such order applies, and

(D) each plan to which such order applies.

(3) **Order may not alter amount, form, etc., of benefits.**—A domestic relations order meets the requirements of this paragraph only if such order—

(A) does not require a plan to provide any type or form of benefit, or any option, not otherwise provided under the plan,

(B) does not require the plan to provide increased benefits (determined on the basis of actuarial value), and

(C) does not require the payment of benefits to an alternate payee which are required to be paid to another alternate payee under another order previously determined to be a qualified domestic relations order.

(4) **Exception for certain payments made after earliest retirement age.**—

(A) In general.—A domestic relations order shall not be treated as failing to meet the requirements of subparagraph (A) of paragraph (3) solely because such order requires that payment of benefits be made to an alternate payee—

(i) in the case of any payment before a participant has separated from service, on or after the date on which the participant attains (or would have attained) the earliest retirement age,

(ii) as if the participant had retired on the date on which such payment is to begin under such order (but taking into account only the present value of the benefits actually accrued and not taking into account the present value of any employer subsidy for early retirement), and

(iii) in any form in which such benefits may be paid under the plan to the participant (other than in the form of a joint and survivor annuity with respect to the alternate payee and his or her subsequent spouse).

For purposes of clause (ii), the interest rate assumption used in determining the present value shall be the interest rate specified in the plan or, if no rate is specified, 5 percent.

(B) Earliest retirement age.—For purposes of this paragraph, the term "earliest retirement age" means the earlier of—

(i) the date on which the participant is entitled to a distribution under the plan, or

(ii) the later of—

(I) the date the participant attains age 50, or

(II) the earliest date on which the participant could begin receiving benefits under the plan if the participant separated from service.

(5) **Treatment of former spouse as surviving spouse for purposes of determining survivor benefits.**—To the extent provided in any qualified domestic relations order—

(A) the former spouse of a participant shall be treated as a surviving spouse of such participant for purposes of Sections 401(a)(11) and 417 (and any spouse of the participant shall not be treated as a spouse of the participant for such purposes), and

(B) if married for at least 1 year, the surviving former spouse shall be treated as meeting the requirements of Section 417(d).

(6) **Plan procedures with respect to orders.**—

(A) Notice and determination by administrator.—In the case of any domestic relations order received by a plan—

(i) the plan administrator shall promptly notify the participant and each alternate payee of the receipt of such order and the plan's procedures for determining the qualified status of domestic relations orders, and

(ii) within a reasonable period after receipt of such order, the plan administrator shall determine whether such order is a qualified domestic relations order and notify the participant and each alternate payee of such determination.

(B) Plan to establish reasonable procedures.—Each plan shall establish reasonable procedures to determine the qualified status of domestic relations orders and to administer distributions under such qualified orders.

(7) **Procedures for period during which determination is being made.**—

(A) In general.—During any period in which the issue of whether a domestic relations order is a qualified domestic relations order is being determined (by the plan administrator, by a court of competent jurisdiction, or otherwise), the plan administrator shall separately account for the amounts (hereinafter in this paragraph referred to as the "segregated amounts") which would have been payable to the alternate payee during such period if the order had been determined to be a qualified domestic relations order.

(B) Payment to alternate payee if order determined to be qualified domestic relations order.—If within the 18-month period described in subparagraph (E) the order (or modification thereof) is determined to be a qualified domestic relations order, the plan administrator shall pay the segregated amounts (including any interest thereon) to the person or persons entitled thereto.

(C) Payment to plan participant in certain cases.—If within the 18-month period described in subparagraph (E)—

(i) it is determined that the order is not a qualified domestic relations order, or

(ii) the issue as to whether such order is a qualified domestic relations order is not resolved, then the plan administrator shall pay the segregated amounts (including any interest thereon) to the person or persons who would have been entitled to such amounts if there had been no order.

(D) Subsequent determination or order to be applied prospectively only.—Any determination that an order is a qualified domestic relations order which is made after the close of the 18-month period described in subparagraph (E) shall be applied prospectively only.

(E) Determination of 18-month period.—For purposes of this paragraph, the 18-month period described in this subparagraph is the 18-month period beginning with the date on which the first payment would be required to be made under the domestic relations order.

(8) **Alternate payee defined.**—The term "alternate payee" means any spouse, former spouse, child or other dependent of a participant who is recognized by a domestic relations order as having a right to receive all, or a portion of, the benefits payable under a plan with respect to such participant.

(9) **Subsection not to apply to plans to which Section 401(a)(13) does not apply.**—This subsection shall not apply to any plan to which Sec-

tion 401(a)(13) does not apply. For purposes of this title, except as provided in regulations, any distribution from an annuity contract under Section 403(b) pursuant to a qualified domestic relations order shall be treated in the same manner as a distribution from a plan to which Section 401(a)(13) applies.

(10) **Waiver of certain distribution requirements.**—With respect to the requirements of subsections (a) and (k) of Section 401, Section 403(b), and Section 409(d), a plan shall not be treated as failing to meet such requirements solely by reason of payments to an alternative payee pursuant to a qualified domestic relations order.

(11) **Application of rules to governmental and church plans.**—For purposes of this title, a distribution or payment from a governmental plan (as defined in subsection (d)) or a church plan (as described in subsection (e)) shall be treated as made pursuant to a qualified domestic relations order if it is made pursuant to a domestic relations order which meets the requirement of clause (i) of paragraph (1)(A).

(12) **Consultation with the Secretary.**—In prescribing regulations under this subsection and Section 401(a)(13), the Secretary of Labor shall consult with the Secretary.

ERISA
Section 206(d)
29 U.S.C. §1056(d)

(d) **Assignment or alienation of plan benefits**

(1) Each pension plan shall provide that benefits provided under the plan may not be assigned or alienated.

(2) For the purposes of paragraph (1) of this subsection, there shall not be taken into account any voluntary and revocable assignment of not to exceed 10 percent of any benefit payment, or of any irrevocable assignment or alienation of benefits executed before September 2, 1974. The preceding sentence shall not apply to any assignment or alienation made for the purposes of defraying plan administration costs. For purposes of this paragraph a loan made to a participant or beneficiary shall not be treated as an assignment or alienation if such loan is secured by the participant's accrued nonforfeitable benefit and is exempt from the tax imposed by Section 4975 of Title 26 (relating to tax on prohibited transactions) by reason of Section 4975(d)(1) of Title 26.

(3)(A) Paragraph (1) shall apply to the creation, assignment, or recognition of a right to any benefit payable with respect to a participant pursuant to a domestic relations order, except that paragraph (1) shall not apply if the order is determined to be a qualified domestic relations order. Each pension plan shall provide for the payment of benefits in accordance with the applicable requirements of any qualified domestic relations order.

(B) For purposes of this paragraph—

(i) the term "qualified domestic relations order" means a domestic relations order—

(I) which creates or recognizes the existence of an alternate payee's right to, or assigns to an alternate payee the right to, receive all or a portion of the benefits payable with respect to a participant under a plan, and

(II) with respect to which the requirements of subparagraphs (C) and (D) are met, and

(ii) the term "domestic relations order" means any judgment, decree, or order (including approval of a property settlement agreement) which—

(I) relates to the provision of child support, alimony payments, or marital property rights to a spouse, former spouse, child, or other dependent of a participant, and

(II) is made pursuant to a State domestic relations law (including a community property law).

(C) A domestic relations order meets the requirements of this subparagraph only if such order clearly specifies—

(i) the name and the last known mailing address (if any) of the participant and the name and mailing address of each alternate payee covered by the order,

(ii) the amount or percentage of the participant's benefits to be paid by the plan to each such alternate payee, or the manner in which such amount or percentage is to be determined,

(iii) the number of payments or period to which such order applies, and

(iv) each plan to which such order applies.

(D) A domestic relations order meets the requirements of this subparagraph only if such order—

(i) does not require a plan to provide any type or form of benefit, or any option, not otherwise provided under the plan,

(ii) does not require the plan to provide increased benefits (determined on the basis of actuarial value), and

(iii) does not require the payment of benefits to an alternate payee which are required to be paid to another alternate payee under another order previously determined to be a qualified domestic relations order.

(E)(i) A domestic relations order shall not be treated as failing to meet the requirements of clause (i) of subparagraph (D) solely because such order requires that payment of benefits be made to an alternate payee—

(I) in the case of any payment before a participant has separated from service, on or after the date on which the participant attains (or would have attained) the earliest retirement age,

(II) as if the participant had retired on the date on which such payment is to begin under such order (but taking into account only the present value of benefits actually accrued and not taking into account the present value of any employer subsidy for early retirement), and

(III) in any form in which such benefits may be paid under the plan to the participant (other than in the form of a joint and survivor annuity with respect to the alternate payee and his or her subsequent spouse).

For purposes of subclause (II), the interest rate assumption used in determining the present value shall be the interest rate specified in the plan or, if no rate is specified, 5 percent.

(ii) For purposes of this subparagraph, the term "earliest retirement age" means the earlier of—

(I) the date on which the participant is entitled to a distribution under the plan, or

(II) the later of the date of the participant attains age 50 or the earliest date on which the participant could begin receiving benefits under the plan if the participant separated from service.

(F) To the extent provided in any qualified domestic relations order—

(i) the former spouse of a participant shall be treated as a surviving spouse of such participant for purposes of Section 1055 (and any spouse of the participant shall not be treated as a spouse of the participant for such purposes) of this title, and

(ii) if married for at least 1 year, the surviving former spouse shall be treated as meeting the requirements of Section 1055(f) of this title.

(G)(i) In the case of any domestic relations order received by a plan—

(I) the plan administrator shall promptly notify the participant and each alternate payee of the receipt of such order and the plan's procedures for determining the qualified status of domestic relations orders, and

(II) within a reasonable period after receipt of such order, the plan administrator shall determine whether such order is a qualified domestic relations order and notify the participant and each alternate payee of such determination.

(ii) Each plan shall establish reasonable procedures to determine the qualified status of domestic relations orders and to administer distributions under such qualified orders. Such procedures—

(I) shall be in writing,

(II) shall provide for the notification of each person specified in a domestic relations order as entitled to payment of benefits under the plan (at the address included in the domestic relations order) of such procedures promptly upon receipt by the plan of the domestic relations order, and

(III) shall permit an alternate payee to designate a representative for receipt of copies of notices that are sent to the alternate payee with respect to a domestic relations order.

(H)(i) During any period in which the issue of whether a domestic relations order is a qualified domestic relations order is being determined (by the plan administrator, by a court of competent jurisdiction, or otherwise), the plan administrator shall separately account for the amounts (hereinafter in this subparagraph referred to as the "segregated amounts") which would have been payable to the alternate payee during such period if the order had been determined to be a qualified domestic relations order.

(ii) If within the 18-month period described in clause (v) the order (or modification thereof) is determined to be a qualified domestic relations order, the plan administrator shall pay the segregated amounts (including any interest thereon) to the person or persons entitled thereto.

(iii) If within the 18-month period described in clause (v)

(I) it is determined that the order is not a qualified domestic relations order, or

(II) the issue as to whether such order is a qualified domestic relations order is not resolved,

then the plan administrator shall pay the segregated amounts (including any interest thereon) to the person or persons who would have been entitled to such amounts if there had been no order.

(iv) Any determination that an order is a qualified domestic relations order which is made after the close of the 18-month period described in clause (v) shall be applied prospectively only.

(v) For purposes of this subparagraph, the 18-month period described in this clause is the 18-month period beginning with the date on which the first payment would be required to be made under the domestic relations order.

(I) If a plan fiduciary acts in accordance with part 4 of this subtitle in—

(i) treating a domestic relations order as being (or not being) a qualified domestic relations order, or

(ii) taking action under subparagraph (H),

then the plan's obligation to the participant and each alternate payee shall be discharged to the extent of any payment made pursuant to such Act.

(J) A person who is an alternate payee under a qualified domestic relations order shall be considered for purposes of any provision of this chapter a beneficiary under the plan. Nothing in the preceding sentence shall permit a requirement under Section 1301 of this title of the payment of more than one premium with respect to a participant for any period.

(K) The term "alternate payee" means any spouse, former spouse, child, or other dependent of a participant who is recognized by a domestic relations order as having a right to receive all, or a portion of, the benefits payable under a plan with respect to such participant.

(L) This paragraph shall not apply to any plan to which paragraph (1) does not apply.

(M) Payment of benefits by a pension plan in accordance with the applicable requirements of a qualified domestic relations order shall not be treated as garnishment for purposes of Section 303(a) of the Consumer Credit Protection Act.

(N) In prescribing regulations under this paragraph, the Secretary shall consult with the Secretary of the Treasury.

Treasury Regulation
Section 1.401(a)-13(g)

(g) **Special rules for qualified domestic relations orders.**

(1) **Definition.**

The term "qualified domestic relations order" (QDRO) has the meaning set forth in Section 414(p). For purposes of the Internal Revenue Code, a QDRO also includes any domestic relations order described in Section 303(d) of the Retirement Equity Act of 1984.

(2) **Plan amendments.**

A plan will not fail to satisfy the qualification requirements of Section 401(a) or 403(a) merely because it does not include provisions with regard to a QDRO.

(3) **Waiver of distribution requirements.**

A plan shall not be treated as failing to satisfy the requirements of Sections 401(a) and (k) and 409(d) solely because of a payment to an alternate payee pursuant to a QDRO. This is the case even if the plan provides for payments pursuant to a QDRO to an alternate payee prior to the time it may make payments to a participant. Thus, for example, a pension plan may pay an alternate payee even though the participant may not receive a distribution because he continues to be employed by the employer.

(4) **Coordination with Section 417.**

(i) **Former spouse.**

(A) **In general.** Under Section 414(p)(5), a QDRO may provide that a former spouse shall be treated as the current spouse of a participant for all or some purposes under Sections 401(a)(11) and 417.

(B) **Consent.**

(1) To the extent a former spouse is treated as the current spouse of the participant by reason of a QDRO, any current spouse shall not be treated as the current spouse. For example, assume H is divorced from W, but a QDRO

provides that H shall be treated as W's current spouse with respect to all of W's benefits under a plan. H will be treated as the surviving spouse under the QPSA and QJSA unless W obtains H's consent to waive the QPSA or QJSA or both. The fact that W married S after W's divorce from H is disregarded. If, however, the QDRO had provided that H shall be treated as W's current spouse only with respect to benefits that accrued prior to the divorce, then H's consent would be needed by W to waive the QPSA or QJSA with respect to benefits accrued before the divorce. S's consent would be required with respect to the remainder of the benefits.

(2) In the preceding examples, if the QDRO ordered that a portion of W's benefit (either through separate accounts or a percentage of the benefit) must be distributed to H rather than ordering that H be treated as W's spouse, the survivor annuity requirements of Sections 401(a)(11) and 417 would not apply to the part of W's benefit awarded H. Instead, the terms of the QDRO would determine how H's portion of W's accrued benefit is paid. W is required to obtain S's consent if W elects to waive either the QJSA or QPSA with respect to the remaining portion of W's benefit.

(C) **Amount of the QPSA or QJSA.**

(1) Where, because of a QDRO, more than one individual is to be treated as the surviving spouse, a plan may provide that the total amount to be paid in the form of a QPSA or survivor portion of a QJSA may not exceed the amount that would be paid if there were only one surviving spouse. The QPSA or survivor portion of the QJSA, as the case may be, payable to each surviving spouse must be paid as an annuity based on the life of each such spouse.

(2) Where the QDRO splits the participant's accrued benefit between the participant and a former spouse (either through separate accounts or percentage of the benefit), the surviving spouse of the participant is entitled to a QPSA or QJSA based on the participant's accrued benefit as of the date of death or the annuity starting date, less the separate account or percentage that is payable to the former spouse. The calculation is made as if the separate account or percentage had been distributed to the participant prior to the relevant date.

(ii) **Current spouse.** Under Section 414(p)(5), even if the applicable election periods (i.e., the first day of the year in which the participant attains age 35 and 90 days before the annuity starting date) have not begun, a QDRO may provide that a current spouse shall not be treated as the current spouse of the participant for all or some purposes under Sections 401(a)(11) and 417. A QDRO may provide that the current spouse waives all future rights to a QPSA or QJSA.

(iii) **Effects on benefits.**

(A) A plan is not required to provide additional vesting or benefits because of a QDRO.

(B) If an alternate payee is treated pursuant to a QDRO as having an interest in the plan benefit, including a separate account or percentage of the participant's account, then the QDRO cannot provide the alternate payee with a greater right to designate a beneficiary for the alternate payee's benefit amount than the participant's right. The QJSA or QPSA provisions of Section 417 do not apply to the spouse of an alternate payee.

(C) If the former spouse who is treated as a current spouse dies prior to the participant's annuity starting date, then any actual current spouse of the participant is treated as the current spouse, except as otherwise provided in a QDRO.

(iv) **Section 415 requirements.** Even though a participant's benefits are awarded to an alternate payee pursuant to a QDRO, the benefits are benefits of the participant for purposes of applying the limitations of Section 415 to the participant's benefits.

Appendix

Legislative History
Retirement Equity Act
P.L. 98-397

C. Assignment or Alienation of Benefits in Divorce, Etc., Distributions (Secs. 104 and 204 of the bill, Sec. 206 of ERISA, and Secs. 401 and 414 of the Code).

Present Law

Generally, under present law, benefits under a pension, profit-sharing, or stock bonus plan (pension plan) are subject to prohibitions against assignment or alienation (spendthrift provisions). Under present law,[21] certain provisions of ERISA supersede (preempt) State laws relating to pension, etc., plans. A plan that does not include these required spendthrift provisions is not a qualified plan under the Code, and State law permitting such an assignment or alienation is generally preempted by ERISA.

Several cases have arisen in which courts have been required to determine whether the ERISA preemption and spendthrift provisions apply to family support obligations (e.g., alimony, separate maintenance, and child support obligations). In some of these cases, the courts have held that ERISA was not intended to preempt State domestic relations law permitting the attachment of vested benefits for the purpose of meeting these obligations.[22] Some courts have held that the ERISA preemption provision does not prevent application of State law permitting attachment of nonvested benefits for the purposes of meeting family support obligations.[23]

There is a divergence of opinion among the courts as to whether ERISA preempts State community property laws insofar as they relate to the rights of a married couple to benefits under a pension, etc., plan.[24]

---

21. Sec. 514 of ERISA.
22. See, e.g., *American Telephone and Telegraph Co. v. Merry*, 592 F.2d 118 (2d Cir. 1979); *Cody v. Riecker*, 594 F.2d 314 (2d Cir. 1979).
23. See, e.g., *Weir v. Weir*, 415 A.2d 638 (1980); *Kikkert v. Kikkert*, 427 A.2d 76 (1981).
24. In *Stone v. Stone*, 633 F.2d 740 (9th Cir. 1980), the court held that ERISA was not intended to preempt community property laws and that a court order requiring a division of retirement benefits did not violate the anti-assignment provisions. In *Francis v. United Technology Corp.*, 458 F.Supp. 84 (N.D. Cal. 1978), however, the court held that ERISA's preemption provision prevents the application of State community property law permitting attachment of plan benefits for family support purposes.

The IRS has ruled that the spendthrift provisions are not violated when a plan trustee complies with a court order requiring the distribution of benefits of a participant in pay status to the participant's spouse or children in order to meet the participant's alimony or child support obligations.[25] The IRS has not taken any position with respect to this issue in cases in which the participant's benefits are not in pay status.

Reasons for Change

The committee believes that the spendthrift rules should be clarified by creating a limited exception that permits benefits under a pension, etc., plan to be divided under certain circumstances. In order to provide rational rules for plan administrators, the committee believes it is necessary to establish guidelines for determining whether the exception to the spendthrift rules applies. In addition, the committee believes that conforming changes to the ERISA preemption provisions are necessary to ensure that only those orders that are excepted from the spendthrift provisions are not preempted by ERISA.

Explanation of Provisions

In general

The bill clarifies the spendthrift provisions by providing new rules for the treatment of certain domestic relations orders. In addition, the bill creates an exception to the ERISA preemption provision with respect to these orders. The bill also provides procedures to be followed by a plan administrator (including the Pension Benefit Guaranty Corporation (PBGC) and an alternate payee (a child, spouse, former spouse, or other dependent of a participant) with respect to domestic relations orders.

Under the bill, if a domestic relations order requires the distribution of all or a part of a participant's benefits under a qualified plan to an alternate payee, then the creation, recognition, or assignment of the alternate payee's right to the benefits is not considered an assignment or alienation of benefits under the plan if and only if the order is a qualified domestic relations order. Because rights created, recognized, or assigned by a qualified domestic relations order, and benefit payments pursuant to such an order, are specifically permitted under the bill, State law providing for these rights and payments under a qualified domestic relations order will continue to be exempt from Federal preemption under ERISA.

---

25. Rev. Rul. 880-27, 1980-1 C.B. 8.

Qualified domestic relations order

Under the bill, the term "qualified domestic relations order" means a domestic relations order that (1) creates or recognizes the existence of an alternate payee's right to, or assigns to an alternate payee the right to, receive all or a portion of the benefits payable with respect to a participant under a pension plan, and (2) meets certain other requirements. A domestic relations order is any judgment, decree, or order (including approval of a property settlement agreement) that relates to the provision of child support, alimony payments, or marital property rights to a spouse, former spouse, child, or other dependent of the participant, and is made pursuant to a State domestic relations law (including community property law). Under the bill, an alternate payee includes any spouse, former spouse, child, or other dependent of a participant who is recognized by a qualified domestic relations order as having a right to receive all, or a portion of, the benefits payable under a plan with respect to the participant.

To be a qualified order, a domestic relations order must clearly specify (1) the name and last known mailing address (if available) of the participant and the name and mailing address of each alternate payee to which the order relates, (2) the amount or percentage of the participant's benefits to be paid to an alternate payee or the manner in which the amount is to be determined, and (3) the number of payments or period for which payments are required. The committee intends that an order will not be treated as failing to be a qualified order merely because the order does not specify the current mailing address of the participant and alternate payee if the plan administrator has reason to know that address independently of the order. For example, if the plan administrator is aware that the alternate payee is also a participant under the plan and the plan records include a current address for each participant, the plan administrator may not treat the order as failing to qualify.

The committee intends that an order that is qualified is to remain qualified with respect to a successor plan of the same employer or a plan of a successor employer (within the meaning of Sec. 414(a)).

A domestic relations order is not a qualified order if it (1) requires a plan to provide any type or form of benefit, or any option, not otherwise provided under the plan, (2) requires the plan to provide increased benefits, or (3) requires payment of benefits to an alternate payee that are required to be paid to another alternate payee under a previously existing qualified domestic relations order. An order does not require a plan to provide increased benefits if the order does not provide for the payment of benefits in excess of the benefits to which the participant would be entitled in the absence of the order.

The bill provides that a domestic relations order is not treated as failing the requirements for a qualified domestic relations order merely because the order provides that payments must begin to the alternate payee on or after the date on which the participant attains the earliest retirement age under the plan whether or not the participant actually retires on that date. If the participant dies before that date, the alternate payee is entitled to benefits only if the qualified domestic relations order requires survivor benefits to be paid. In the case of an order providing for the payment of benefits after the earliest retirement age, the payments to the alternate payee at that time are computed as if the participant had retired on the date on which benefit payments commence under the order.

When payments are made to an alternate payee before the participant retires, the payments are computed by taking into account only benefits actually accrued and not taking into account any employer subsidy for early retirement. The amount to be paid to the alternate payee is to be calculated by using the participant's normal retirement benefit accrued as of the date payout begins and by actuarially reducing such benefit based on the interest rate specified in the plan or 5 percent, if the plan does not specify an interest rate. A plan providing only normal and subsidized early retirement benefits would not specify a rate for determining actuarially equivalent, unsubsidized benefits.

If an alternate payee begins to receive benefits under the order and the participant subsequently retires with subsidized early retirement benefits, the order may specify that the amount payable to the alternate payee is to be recalculated so that the alternate payee also receives a share of the subsidized benefit to which the participant is entitled. The payment of early retirement benefits with respect to a participant who has not yet retired or the increase in benefits payable to the alternate payee after the recalculation is not to be considered to violate the prohibition for increased benefits.

The payments to the alternate payee after the earliest retirement date may be paid in any form permitted under the plan (other than a joint and survivor annuity with respect to the alternate payee and the alternate payee's spouse). In the case of a defined contribution plan, the earliest retirement date is the date on which the participant attains an age that is 10 years before the normal retirement age.

Under the bill, a plan is not treated as failing to satisfy the requirements of Section 401(a), 409(d), or 401(k) of the Internal Revenue Code that prohibit payment of benefits prior to termination of employment solely because the plan makes payments to the alternate payee in accordance with a qualified domestic relations order.

Under the bill, an alternate payee is treated as a beneficiary for all purposes under the plan. In no event, however, will more than one PBGC premium be collected with respect to the participant's benefits (determined as if a qualified domestic relations order had not been issued) even though such benefits, subject to the usual limits, may be guaranteed by the PBGC.

Determination by plan administrator

Under the bill, the administrator of a plan that receives a domestic relations order is required to notify promptly the participant and any other alternate payee of receipt of the order and the plan's procedures for determining whether the order is qualified. In addition, within a reasonable period after receipt of the order, the plan administrator is to determine whether the order is qualified and notify the participant and alternate payee of the determination. The notices required under these rules are to be sent to the addresses specified in the order or, if the order fails to specify an address, to the last known address of the participant or alternate payee known to the plan administrator.

The bill authorizes the Secretary of Labor to prescribe regulations defining the reasonable period during which the plan administrator is to determine whether an order is qualified. In addition, the bill provides that plans are to establish reasonable procedures to determine whether domestic relations orders are qualified and to administer distributions under qualified domestic relations orders. Ordinarily, a plan need not be amended to implement the domestic relations provisions of the bill.

Deferral of benefit payments

During any period in which the issue of whether a domestic relations order is a qualified order is being determined (by the plan administrator, by a court of competent jurisdiction, or otherwise), the plan administrator is to defer the payment of any benefits in dispute. These deferred benefits are segregated either in a separate account in the plan or in an escrow account. In the case of a defined benefit plan, the amounts are to be placed in an escrow account. Of course, segregation is not required for amounts that would not otherwise be paid during the period of the dispute.

If the order is determined to be a qualified domestic relations order within

18 months after the deferral of benefits, the plan administrator is to pay the segregated amounts (plus interest) to the persons entitled to receive them. If the plan administrator determines that the order is not a qualified order, or, after the 18-month period has expired, has not resolved the issue of whether the order is qualified, the segregated amounts are paid to the person or persons who would have received the amounts if the order had not been issued.

Any determination that an order is qualified after expiration of the 18-month period is to be applied prospectively. Thus, the plan administrator determines that the order is qualified after the 18-month period, the plan is not liable for payments to the alternate payee for the period before the order is determined to be qualified.

Of course, the provisions of the bill do not affect any cause of action that an alternate payee may have against the participant. For example, if an order is determined to be qualified after the 18-month period, the alternate payee may have a cause of action under State law against the participant for amounts paid to the participant that should have been paid to the alternate payee.

During any period in which the alternate payee cannot be located, the plan is not permitted to provide for the forfeiture of the amounts that would have been paid unless the plan provides for full reinstatement when the alternate payee is located.

Consultation with the Secretary of the Treasury

Under the bill, the Secretary of Labor is required to consult with the Secretary of the Treasury in prescribing regulations under these provisions.

Tax treatment of divorce distributions

The bill provides rules for determining the tax treatment of benefits subject to a qualified domestic relations order. Under the bill, for purposes of determining the taxability of benefits, the alternate payee is treated as a distributee with respect to payments received from or under a plan.

Under the bill, net employee contributions, (together with other amounts treated as the participant's investment in the contract) are apportioned between the participant and the alternate payee under regulations prescribed by the Secretary of the Treasury. The apportionment is to be made pro rata, on the basis of the present value of all benefits of the alternate payee under the plan (as alternate payee with respect to the participant under a qualified domestic relations order).

Payments to an alternate payee before the participant attains age 59½ are not subject to the 10 percent additional income tax that would otherwise apply under certain circumstances if the participant received the amounts.

The bill provides that the interest of the alternate payee is not taken into account in determining whether a distribution to the participant is a lump sum distribution. Under the bill, benefits distributed to an alternate payee under a qualified domestic relations order can be rolled over, tax-free, to an individual retirement account or to an individual retirement annuity. The usual income tax rules apply to benefits not rolled over. The special rules for lump sum distributions from qualified plans will not apply to benefits distributed to an alternate payee.

Effective Dates

The provisions of the bill relating to assignments in divorce, etc., proceedings generally apply on January 1, 1985. If a domestic relations order was received by a plan before the date of enactment, however, the plan administrator is to treat the order as a qualified domestic relations order to the extent payments are being made pursuant to the order. In addition, the plan administrator may treat any other order entered before the effective date as a qualified order. The committee encourages plan administrators to treat an existing order as qualified to the extent it is consistent with the provisions of the bill. Of course, if the plan administrator does not treat an order as qualified, the alternate payee may amend the order to satisfy the requirements for a qualified order.

IRS Notice 97-11
Sample Language for a Qualified Domestic Relations Order

I. Purpose

(1) This Notice provides information intended to assist domestic relations attorneys, plan participants, spouses and former spouses of participants, and plan administrators in drafting and reviewing a qualified domestic relations order (QDRO). The Notice provides sample language that may be included in a QDRO relating to a plan that is qualified under Section 401(a) or Section 403(a) of the Internal Revenue Code of 1986 (qualified plan or plan) and that is subject to Section 401(a)(13). The Notice also discusses a number of issues that should be considered in drafting a QDRO. A QDRO is a domestic relations order that provides for payment of benefits from a qualified plan to a spouse, former spouse, child or other dependent of a plan participant and that meets certain requirements.

A. Statutory QDRO Requirements

(2) Section 401(a)(13)(A) of the Code provides that benefits under a qualified plan may not be assigned or alienated. Section 401(a)(13)(B) establishes an exception to the antialienation rule for assignments made pursuant to domestic relations orders that constitute QDROs within the meaning of Section 414(p). A "domestic relations order" is defined in Section 414(p)(1)(B) as any judgment, decree, or order (including approval of a property settlement agreement) that (i) relates to the provision of child support, alimony payments, or marital property rights to a spouse, former spouse, child, or other dependent of a participant, and (ii) is made pursuant to a State domestic relations law (including a community property law). There is no exception to the Section 401(a)(13)(A) antialienation rule for assignments made pursuant to domestic relations orders that are not QDROs.

(3) Section 414(p)(1)(A) provides, in general, that a QDRO is a domestic relations order that creates or recognizes the existence of an alternate payee's right, or assigns to an alternate payee the right, to receive all or a portion of the benefits payable with respect to a participant under a plan, and that meets the requirements of paragraphs (2) and (3) of Section 414(p). Section 414(p)(2) requires that a QDRO clearly specify: (A) the name and last known mailing address (if any) of the participant and of each alternate payee covered by the

order, (B) the amount or percentage of the participant's benefits to be paid by the plan to each alternate payee, or the manner in which that amount or percentage is to be determined,(C) the number of payments or period to which the order applies, and (D) each plan to which the order applies.

(4) Section 414(p)(3) provides that a QDRO cannot require a plan to provide any type or form of benefit, or any option, not otherwise provided under the plan; cannot require a plan to provide increased benefits (determined on the basis of actuarial value); and cannot require the payment of benefits to an alternate payee that are required to be paid to another alternate payee under another order previously determined to be a QDRO. Section 414(p)(4)(A)(i) provides that a domestic relations order shall not be treated as failing to meet the requirements of Section 414(p)(3)(A) (and thus will not fail to be a QDRO) solely because the order requires payment of benefits to an alternate payee on or after the participant's earliest retirement age, even if the participant has not separated from service at that time. Section 414(p)(4)(B) defines earliest retirement age as the earlier of (i) the date on which the participant is entitled to a distribution under the plan, or (ii) the later of (I) the date the participant attains age 50, or (II) the earliest date on which the participant could begin receiving benefits under the plan if the participant separated from service.

(5) Section 414(p)(5) permits a QDRO to provide that the participant's former spouse shall be treated as the participant's surviving spouse for purposes of Sections 401(a)(11) and 417 (relating to the right to receive survivor benefits and requirements concerning consent to distributions), and that any other spouse of the participant shall not be treated as a spouse of the participant for these purposes. An alternate payee is defined under Section 414(p)(8) as any spouse, former spouse, child or other dependent of a participant who is recognized by a domestic relations order as having a right to receive all, or a portion of, the benefits payable under a plan with respect to the participant. Section 414(p)(10) provides that a plan shall not fail to satisfy the requirements of Sections 401(a), 401(k) or 403(b) solely by reason of payments made to an alternate payee pursuant to a QDRO.

B. Small Business Job Protection Act of 1996

(6) Section 1457(a)(2) of the Small Business Job Protection Act of 1996 (SBJPA) directs the Secretary of the Treasury (Secretary) to develop sample language for inclusion in a form for a QDRO described in Section 414(p)(1)(A) of the Code and Section 206(d)(3)(B)(i) of the Employee Retirement Income Security Act of 1974 (ERISA) that meets the requirements contained in those

sections, and the provisions of which focus attention on the need to consider the treatment of any lump sum payment, qualified joint and survivor annuity (QJSA), or qualified preretirement survivor annuity (QPSA). Accordingly, the Service and Treasury are publishing the discussion and sample QDRO language set forth in the Appendix to this Notice.

(7) Section 1457(a)(1) of the SBJPA directs the Secretary to publish sample language that can be included in a form that is used for a spouse to consent to a participant's waiver of a QJSA or QPSA. This sample language for use in spousal consent forms is contained in Notice 97-10 in this Bulletin.

C. Department of Labor Interpretive Authority

(8) Section 206(d)(3) of ERISA (29 U.S.C. Section 1056(d)(3)) contains QDRO provisions that are substantially parallel to those of Section 414(p) of the Code. The Department of Labor has jurisdiction to interpret these provisions (except to the extent provided in Section 401(n) of the Code) and the provisions governing the fiduciary duties owed with respect to domestic relations orders and QDROs. Section 401(n) gives the Secretary of the Treasury the authority to prescribe rules or regulations necessary to coordinate the requirements of Sections 401(a)(13) and 414(p), and the regulations issued by the Department of Labor thereunder, with other Code provisions. The Department of Labor has reviewed this Notice, including its Appendix, and has advised the Service and Treasury that the discussion and sample language are consistent with the views of the Department of Labor concerning the statutory requirements for QDROs. This Notice, including its Appendix, is not intended by the Service or Treasury to convey interpretations of the statutory requirements applicable to QDROs, but only to provide examples of language that may be (but are not required to be) used in drafting a QDRO that satisfies these requirements.

II. Sample Language

(9) The Appendix to this Notice has two parts. Part I discusses certain issues that should be considered when drafting a QDRO. Part II contains sample language that will assist in drafting a QDRO. Drafters who use the sample language will need to conform it to the terms of the retirement plan to which the QDRO applies, and to specify the amounts assigned and other terms of the QDRO so as to achieve an appropriate division of marital property or level of family support. A domestic relations order is not required to incorporate the sample language in order to satisfy the requirements for a QDRO, and a domestic relations order that incorporates part of the sample language may omit or modify other parts.

(10) The sample language addresses a variety of matters, but is not designed to address all retirement benefit issues that may arise in each domestic relations matter or QDRO. Further, some of the sample language, while helpful in facilitating the administration of a QDRO, is not necessarily required for the order to satisfy the requirements for a QDRO. Alternative formulations would be permissible for use in drafting orders that meet the statutory requirements for a QDRO.

III. Other Sources of Information

(11) The Pension Benefit Guaranty Corporation (PBGC) recently published a booklet entitled "Divorce Orders & PBGC," which discusses the special QDRO rules that apply for plans that have been terminated and are trusteed by PBGC, and provides model QDROs for use with those plans. This publication may be obtained by calling PBGC's Customer Service Center at 1-800-400-PBGC or electronically via the PBGC Internet site at http://www.pbgc.gov.

(12) Additional information on the rights of participants and spouses to plan benefits can be found in a two-booklet set published by the Service, entitled "Looking Out for #2." These booklets discuss retirement benefit choices under a defined contribution or a defined benefit plan, and may be obtained by calling the Internal Revenue Service at 1-800-TAX-FORM, and asking for Publication 1565 (defined contribution plans) or Publication 1566 (defined benefit plans).

IV. Comments

(13) The Service invites the public to comment on the QDRO discussion and sample language included in the Appendix to this Notice, and welcomes suggestions concerning possible additional sample language. Comments may be submitted to the Internal Revenue Service at CC:DOM:CORP:R (Notice 97-11), Room 5226, Internal Revenue Service, POB 7604, Ben Franklin Station, Washington, D.C. 20044. Alternatively, taxpayers may hand-deliver comments between the hours of 8 a.m. and 5 p.m. to CC:DOM:CORP:R (Notice 97-11), Courier's desk, Internal Revenue Service, 1111 Constitution Ave., N.W., Washington, D.C., or may submit comments electronically via the IRS Internet site at http://www.irs.ustreas.gov/prod/ tax_regs/comments.html.

Drafting Information

(14) The principal authors of this Notice are Diane S. Bloom of the Employee Plans Division and Susan M. Lennon of the Office of the Associate Chief

Counsel (Employee Benefits and Exempt Organizations); however, other personnel from the Service and Treasury contributed to its development. For further information regarding this Notice, please contact the Employee Plans Division's taxpayer assistance telephone service at (202) 622-6074/6075, between the hours of 1:30 p.m. and 4 p.m. Eastern Time, Monday through Thursday. Alternatively, please call Ms. Bloom at (202) 622-6214 or Ms. Lennon at (202) 622-4606. Questions concerning QDROs may be addressed to Susan G. Lahne of the Pension and Welfare Benefits Administration, Department of Labor, at (202) 219-7461. These telephone numbers are not toll-free.

Appendix to 97-11

(15) Part I of this Appendix discusses certain issues that are relevant in drafting a qualified domestic relations order (QDRO). Part II of this Appendix contains sample language that can be used in a QDRO. However, the discussion and sample language do not attempt to address every issue that may arise in drafting a QDRO. Also, some parts of the discussion are not relevant to all situations and some parts of the sample language are not appropriate for all QDROs. In formulating a particular QDRO, it is important that the drafters tailor the QDRO to the needs of the parties and ensure that the QDRO is consistent with the terms of the retirement plan to which the QDRO applies.

Part I. Discussion of QDRO Requirements and Related Issues

(16) In order to be recognized as a QDRO, an order must first be a "domestic relations order." A domestic relations order is any judgment, decree or order (including approval of a property settlement) which (i) relates to the provision of child support, alimony payments or marital property rights to a spouse, former spouse, child or other dependent of the plan participant, and (ii) is made pursuant to a State domestic relations law (including a community property law). A State authority must actually issue an order or formally approve a proposed property settlement before it can be a domestic relations order. A property settlement signed by a participant and the participant's former spouse or a draft order to which both parties consent is not a domestic relations order until the State authority has adopted it as an order or formally approved it and made it part of the domestic relations proceeding.

(17) The sample language in Part II assumes that the QDRO applies to one qualified plan and one alternate payee. If a QDRO is intended to cover more than one qualified plan or alternate payee, the QDRO should clearly state which qualified plan and which alternate payee each provision is intended to address.

(18) The terms of a qualified plan must be set forth in a written document. The plan must also establish written QDRO procedures to be used by the plan administrator in determining whether a domestic relations order is a QDRO and in administering QDROs. The plan administrator maintains copies of the plan document and the plan's QDRO procedures. If the plan is required under federal law to have a summary plan description (SPD), the plan administrator will also have a copy of the SPD. The information in these documents is helpful in drafting a QDRO. The drafter of a QDRO may wish to obtain copies of these documents before drafting a QDRO.

A. Identification of Participant and Alternate Payee

(19) A QDRO must clearly specify the name and last known mailing address (if any) of the participant and of each alternate payee covered by the QDRO. In the event that an alternate payee is a minor or legally incompetent, the QDRO should also include the name and address of the alternate payee's legal representative. A QDRO can have more than one alternate payee, such as a former spouse and a child.

(20) The "participant" is the individual whose benefits under the plan are being divided by the QDRO. The participant's spouse (or former spouse, child, or other dependent) who receives some or all of the plan's benefits with respect to the participant under the terms of the QDRO is the "alternate payee."

B. Identification of Retirement Plan

(21) A QDRO must clearly identify each plan to which the QDRO applies. A QDRO can satisfy this requirement by stating the full name of the plan as provided in the plan document.

C. Amount of Benefits to Be Paid to Alternate Payee

(22) A QDRO must clearly specify the amount or percentage of the participant's benefits in the plan that is assigned to each alternate payee, or the manner in which the amount or percentage is to be determined. Many factors should be taken into account in determining which benefits to assign to an alternate payee and how these benefits are to be assigned. The following discussion highlights some of these factors. Because of the complexity and variety of the factors that should be considered, and the need to tailor the assignment of benefits under a QDRO to the individual circumstances of the parties, specific sample language regarding the assignment of benefits has not been provided in Part II of this Appendix.

1. Types of Benefits

(23) In order to decide how to divide benefits under a QDRO, the drafter first should determine the types of benefits the plan provides. Most benefits provided by qualified plans can be classified as (1) retirement benefits that are paid during the participant's life and (2) survivor benefits that are paid to beneficiaries after the participant's death. Generally, a QDRO can assign all or a portion of each of these types of benefits to an alternate payee. The drafters of a QDRO should coordinate the assignment of these types of benefits. QDRO drafters should also consider how the benefits divided under the QDRO may be affected, under the plan, by the death of either the participant or the alternate payee.

2. Types of Qualified Plans

(24) Another important factor to consider in the drafting of a QDRO is the type of plan to which the QDRO will apply. As discussed below, the type of plan may affect the types of benefits available for assignment, how the parties choose to assign the benefits, and other matters.

(25) There are two basic types of qualified plans to which QDROs apply: defined benefit plans and defined contribution plans.

a. Defined Benefit Plans

(26) A "defined benefit plan" promises to pay each participant a specific benefit at retirement. The basic retirement benefits are usually based on a formula that takes into account factors such as the number of years a participant has worked for the employer and the participant's salary. The basic retirement benefits are generally expressed in the form of periodic payments for the participant's life beginning at the plan's normal retirement age. This stream of periodic payments is generally known as an "annuity." There are special rules that apply if the participant is married; these rules are discussed in greater detail below. A plan may also provide that these retirement benefits may be paid in other forms, such as a lump sum payment.

b. Defined Contribution Plans

(27) A "defined contribution plan" is a retirement plan that provides for an individual account for each participant. The participant's benefits are based solely on the amount contributed to the participant's account, and any income, expenses, gains and losses, and any forfeitures of accounts of other participants

which may be allocated to such participant's account. Examples of defined contribution plans include a profit sharing plan (including a 401(k) plan), an employee stock ownership plan (an ESOP) and a money purchase pension plan. Defined contribution plans commonly permit retirement benefits to be paid in the form of a lump sum payment of the participant's entire account balance.

3. Approaches to Dividing Retirement Benefits

(28) There are two common approaches to dividing retirement benefits in a QDRO: one awards a separate interest in the retirement benefits to the alternate payee, and the other allows the alternate payee to share in the payment of the retirement benefits. In drafting a QDRO using either of these approaches, consideration should be given to factors such as whether the plan is a defined benefit plan or defined contribution plan, and the purpose of the QDRO (such as whether the QDRO is meant to provide spousal support or child support, or to divide marital property).

a. Separate Interest Approach

(29) A QDRO that creates a "separate interest" divides the participant's benefits into two separate parts: one for the participant and one for the alternate payee. Subject to the terms of the plan and as discussed in more detail below, a QDRO may provide that the alternate payee can determine the form in which his or her benefits are paid and when benefit payments commence. If benefits are allocated under the separate interest approach, the drafters of a QDRO should take into account certain issues depending on the type of plan.

(1) Issues Relevant to Defined Benefit Plans

(30) The treatment of subsidies provided by a plan and the treatment of future increases in benefits due to increases in the participant's compensation, additional years of service, or changes in the plan's provisions are among the matters that should be considered when drafting a QDRO that uses the separate interest approach to allocate benefits under a defined benefit plan.

(31) **Subsidies:** Defined benefit plans may promise to pay benefits at various times and in alternative forms. Benefits paid at certain times or in certain forms may have a greater actuarial value than the basic retirement benefits payable at normal retirement age. When one form of benefit has a greater actuarial value than another form, the difference in value is often called a subsidy. Plans usually provide that a participant must meet specific eligibility re-

quirements, such as working for a minimum number of years for the employer that maintains the plan, in order to receive the subsidy.

(32) For example, a defined benefit plan may offer an "early retirement subsidy" to employees who retire before the plan's normal retirement age but after having worked for a specific number of years for the employer maintaining the plan. In some cases, this subsidized benefit provides payments in the form of an annuity that pays the same annual amount as would be paid if the payments commenced instead at the normal retirement age. Because these benefits are not reduced for early commencement, they have a greater actuarial value than benefits payable at normal retirement age. This subsidy may be available only for certain forms of benefit.

(33) A QDRO may award to the alternate payee all or part of the participant's basic retirement benefits. A QDRO can also address the disposition of any subsidy to which the participant may become entitled after the QDRO has been entered.

(34) **Future Increases in the Participant's Benefits:** A participant's basic retirement benefits may increase due to circumstances that occur after a QDRO has been entered, such as increases in salary, crediting of additional years of service, or amendments to the plan's provisions, including amendments to provide cost of living adjustments. The treatment of such benefit increases should be considered when drafting a QDRO using the separate interest approach.

(2) Issues Relevant to Defined Contribution Plans

(35) Investment of the amount assigned to the alternate payee when the account is invested in more than one investment vehicle and division of any future allocation of contributions or forfeitures to the participant's account are among the matters that should be considered when drafting a QDRO that allocates the alternate payee a separate interest under a defined contribution plan.

(36) **Investment Choices:** The participant's account may be invested in more than one investment fund. If the plan provides for participant-directed investment of the participant's account, consideration should be given to how the alternate payee's interest will be invested.

(37) **Future Allocations:** A participant's account balance may later increase due to the allocation of contributions or forfeitures after the QDRO has been entered. A QDRO may provide that the amounts assigned to the alternate payee will include a portion of such future allocations.

b. Shared Payment Approach

(38) A QDRO may use the "shared payment" approach, under which benefit payments from the plan are split between the participant and the alternate payee. The alternate payee receives payments under this approach only when the participant receives payments. A QDRO may provide that the alternate payee will commence receiving benefit payments when the participant begins receiving payments or at a later stated date, and that the alternate payee will cease to share in the benefit payments at a stated date (or upon a stated event, provided that adequate notice is given to the plan). In splitting the benefit payments, the QDRO may award the alternate payee either a percentage or a dollar amount of each of the participant's benefit payments; in either case, the amount awarded cannot exceed the amount of each payment to which the participant is entitled under the plan. If a QDRO awards a percentage of the participant's benefit payments (rather than a dollar amount), then, unless the QDRO provides otherwise, the alternate payee generally will automatically receive a share of any future subsidy or other increase in the participant's benefits.

D. Form and Commencement of Payment to Alternate Payee

(39) QDRO drafters should take into account certain issues that may arise in connection with the alternate payee's choice of a form of benefit payments and the date on which payment will commence.

1. Separate Interest Approach

a. Form of alternate payee's benefit payments

(40) A QDRO either may specify a particular form in which payments are to be made to the alternate payee or may provide that the alternate payee may choose a form of benefit from among the options available to the participant. However, federal law provides that the alternate payee cannot receive payments in the form of a joint and survivor annuity with respect to the alternate payee and his or her subsequent spouse.

(41) The choice of the form of benefits should take into account the period over which payments will be made. For example, if the alternate payee elects to receive a lump sum payment, no further payments will be made by the plan with respect to the alternate payee's interest.

(42) Any decision concerning the form of benefit should take into account the difference, if any, in the actuarial value of different benefit forms available

under the plan. For example, as discussed above, a plan might provide an early retirement subsidy that is available only for payment in certain forms.

(43) In addition, the forms of benefit available to the alternate payee may be limited by Section 401(a)(9) of the Code, which specifies the date by which benefit payments from a qualified plan must commence and limits the period over which the benefit payments may be made. Section 1.401(a)(9)-1, Q&A H-4, of the Proposed Income Tax Regulations addresses the application of the required minimum distribution rules of Section 401(a)(9) to payments to an alternate payee. The proposed regulation limits the period over which benefits may be paid with respect to the alternate payee's interest. For example, the proposed regulation provides that distribution of the alternate payee's separate interest will not satisfy Section 401(a)(9)(A)(ii) of the Code if the separate interest is distributed over the joint lives of the alternate payee and a designated beneficiary (other than the participant).

b. Commencement of benefit payments to alternate payee

(44) Under the separate interest approach, the alternate payee may begin receiving benefits at a different time than the participant. A QDRO either may specify a time at which payments are to commence to the alternate payee or may provide that the alternate payee can elect a time when benefits will commence in accordance with the terms of the plan. In two circumstances, an alternate payee who is given a separate interest may begin receiving his or her separate benefit before the participant is eligible to begin receiving payments. First, federal law provides that benefit payments to the alternate payee may begin as soon as the participant attains his or her earliest retirement age. Federal law defines "earliest retirement age" as the earlier of (i) the date on which the participant is entitled to a distribution under the plan, or (ii) the later of (I) the date the participant attains age 50, or (II) the earliest date on which the participant could begin receiving benefits under the plan if the participant separated from service. Second, the retirement plan may (but is not required to) allow payments to begin to an alternate payee at a date before the earliest retirement date.

2. Shared Payment Approach

(45) As indicated above, under the shared payment approach, benefit payments are split between the participant and the alternate payee. The alternate payee receives payments in the same form as the participant. Further, payments to the alternate payee do not commence before the participant has

begun to receive benefits. Payments to the alternate payee can cease at any time stated in the QDRO but do not continue after payments with respect to the participant cease. As noted above, a QDRO must state the number of payments or the period to which the order applies.

E. Survivor Benefits and Treatment of Former Spouse as Participant's Spouse

(46) Survivor benefits include both benefits payable to surviving spouses and other benefits that are payable after the participant's death. These benefits can be awarded to an alternate payee. In determining the assignment of survivor benefits, QDRO drafters should take into account that benefits awarded to the alternate payee under a QDRO will not be available to a subsequent spouse of the participant or to another beneficiary. QDRO drafters may consult with the plan administrator for information on the survivor benefits provided under the plan.

(47) A QDRO may provide for treatment of a former spouse of a participant as the participant's spouse with respect to all or a portion of the spousal survivor benefits that must be provided under federal law. The following discussion explains the spousal survivor benefits that must be offered under a plan, and identifies issues that should be considered in determining whether to treat the alternate payee as the participant's spouse.

(48) Only a spouse or former spouse of the participant can be treated as a spouse under a QDRO. A child or other dependent who is an alternate payee under a QDRO cannot be treated as the spouse of a participant.

(49) Retirement plans generally need not provide the special survivor benefits to the participant's surviving spouse unless the participant is married for at least one year. If the retirement plan to which the QDRO relates contains such a one-year marriage requirement, then the QDRO cannot require that the alternate payee be treated as the participant's spouse if the marriage lasted for less than one year.

1. Qualified Joint and Survivor Annuity

(50) Federal law generally requires that defined benefit plans and certain defined contribution plans pay retirement benefits to participants who were married on the participant's annuity starting date (this is the first day of the first period for which an amount is payable to the participant) in a special form called a qualified joint and survivor annuity (QJSA). Under a QJSA, retirement payments are made monthly (or at other regular intervals) to the par-

ticipant for his or her lifetime; after the participant dies, the plan pays the participant's surviving spouse an amount each month (or other regular interval) that is at least one half of the retirement benefit that was paid to the participant. At any time that benefits are permitted to commence under the plan, a QJSA must be offered that commences at the same time and that has an actuarial value that is at least as great as any other form of benefit payable under the plan at the same time. A married participant can choose to receive retirement benefits in a form other than a QJSA if the participant's spouse agrees in writing to that choice.

2. Qualified Preretirement Survivor Annuity

(51) Federal law generally requires that defined benefit plans and certain defined contribution plans pay a monthly survivor benefit to a surviving spouse for the spouse's life when a married participant dies prior to the participant's annuity starting date, to the extent the participant's benefit is nonforfeitable under the terms of the plan at the time of his or her death. This benefit is called a qualified preretirement survivor annuity, or QPSA. As a general rule, an individual loses the right to the QPSA survivor benefits when he or she is divorced from the participant. However, if a former spouse is treated as the participant's surviving spouse under a QDRO, the former spouse is eligible to receive the QPSA unless the former spouse consents to the waiver of the QPSA. If the spouse does not waive the QPSA, the plan may allow the spouse to receive the value of the QPSA in a form other than an annuity.

3. Defined Contribution Plans Not Subject to the QJSA or QPSA Requirements

(52) Those defined contribution plans that are not required to pay benefits to married participants in the form of a QJSA or a QPSA are required by federal law to pay the balance remaining in the participant's account after the participant dies to the participant's surviving spouse. If the spouse gives written consent, the participant can direct that upon his or her death the account will be paid to a beneficiary other than the spouse, for example, the couple's children.

4. Alternate Payee Treated as Spouse

(53) A QDRO may provide that an alternate payee who is a former spouse of the participant will be treated as the participant's spouse for some or all of the benefits payable upon the participant's death, so that the alter-

nate payee will receive benefits provided to a spouse under the plan. To the extent that a former spouse is to be treated under the plan as the participant's spouse pursuant to a QDRO, any subsequent spouse of the participant cannot be treated as the participant's surviving spouse. Thus, QDRO drafters should consider the potential impact of designating a former spouse as the participant's spouse on the disposition of survivor benefits among the former spouse and any subsequent spouse of the participant, as well as the impact on children or any other beneficiaries designated by the participant in accordance with the terms of the plan.

(54) In determining the portion of the participant's benefits for which the alternate payee is treated as the spouse, the drafters should take into account the manner in which benefits are otherwise divided under the QDRO. In particular, consideration should be given to whether the formula for dividing the participant's benefits for this purpose should be coordinated with the formula otherwise used for dividing the benefits.

(55) Under a defined benefit plan, or a defined contribution plan that is subject to the QJSA and QPSA requirements, to the extent the former spouse is treated as the current spouse, the former spouse must consent to payment of retirement benefits in a form other than a QJSA or to the participant's waiver of the QPSA. For example, in a defined benefit plan, the participant would not be able to elect to receive a lump sum payment of the retirement benefits for which the alternate payee is treated as the participant's spouse unless the alternate payee consents. Similarly, the former spouse's consent might be required for any loan to the participant from the plan that is secured by his or her retirement benefits. In a defined contribution plan that is not subject to the QJSA and QPSA requirements, to the extent the QDRO treats the former spouse as the participant's spouse under the plan, the survivor benefits under the plan must be paid to the former spouse unless he or she consents to have those benefits paid to someone else.

F. Tax Treatment of Benefit Payments Made Pursuant to a QDRO

(56) The federal income tax treatment of retirement benefits is governed by federal law, and a QDRO cannot designate who will be liable for the taxes owed when retirement benefits are paid. For a description of the tax consequences of payments to an alternate payee pursuant to a QDRO, see Internal Revenue Service Publication 575, "Pension and Annuity Income." A local IRS office can provide this publication, or it may be obtained by calling 1-800-TAX-FORM.

Part II. Sample Language for Inclusion in QDRO

A. Sample Language for Identification of Participant and Alternate Payee

(57) The "Participant" is [insert name of Participant]. The Participant's address is [insert Participant's address]. The Participant's Social Security number is [insert participant's Social Security number].

(58) The "Alternate Payee" is [insert name of Alternate Payee]. The Alternate Payee's address is [insert Alternate Payee's address]. The Alternate Payee's Social Security number is [insert Alternate Payee's Social Security number]. The Alternate Payee is the [describe the Alternate Payee's relationship to Participant] of the Participant.

B. Sample Language for Identification of Retirement Plan

(59) This order applies to benefits under the [insert formal name of retirement plan] (Plan).

C. Amount of Benefits to Be Paid to Alternate Payee

Instruction: The QDRO should clearly specify the amount or percentage of benefits assigned to the Alternate Payee or the manner in which the amount or percentage is to be determined, and the number of payments or period to which the Order applies. There are many different forms in which benefits may be paid from a qualified plan. Because of the diversity of factors that should be considered, and the need to tailor the assignment of benefits under a QDRO to meet the needs of the parties involved, specific sample language regarding the assignment of benefits has not been provided. See the discussion in Part I for further information.

D. Sample Language for Form and Commencement of Payment to Alternate Payee

Instruction: Drafters using the separate interest approach may use paragraph 1. Drafters using the shared payment approach may use paragraph 2. Drafters using the separate interest approach for a portion of the benefits allocated to the alternate payee and the shared payment approach for the remainder should modify the sample language to specify the benefits to which each paragraph provided below applies.

1. *Separate Interest Approach*

(60) The Alternate Payee may elect to receive payment from the Plan of

the benefits assigned to the Alternate Payee under this Order in any form in which such benefits may be paid under the Plan to the Participant (other than in the form of a joint and survivor annuity with respect to the Alternate Payee and his or her subsequent spouse), but only if the form elected complies with the minimum distribution requirements of Section 401(a)(9) of the Internal Revenue Code. Payments to the Alternate Payee pursuant to this Order shall commence on any date elected by the Alternate Payee (and such election shall be made in accordance with the terms of the Plan), but not earlier than the Participant's earliest retirement age (or such earlier date as allowed under the terms of the Plan), and not later than the earlier of (A) the date the Participant would be required to commence benefits under the terms of the Plan or (B) the latest date permitted by Section 401(a)(9) of the Internal Revenue Code. For purposes of this Order, the Participant's earliest retirement age shall be the earlier of (i) the date on which the participant is entitled to a distribution under the Plan, or (ii) the later of (I) the date the Participant attains age 50, or (II) the earliest date on which the Participant could begin receiving benefits under the plan if the Participant separated from service.

2. Shared Payment Approach

(61) The Alternate Payee shall receive payments from the Plan of the benefits assigned to the Alternate Payee under this Order (including payments attributable to the period in which the issue of whether this Order is a qualified domestic relations order is being determined) commencing as soon as practicable after this Order has been determined to be a qualified domestic relations order or, if later, on the date the Participant commences receiving benefit payments from the Plan. Payment to the Alternate Payee shall cease on the earlier of: [insert date or future event, such as the Alternate Payee's remarriage], or the date that payments from the Plan with respect to the Participant cease.

E. Sample Language for Treatment of Former Spouse as Participant's Spouse

Instruction: The Alternate Payee may be treated as the Participant's spouse only if the Alternate Payee is the Participant's spouse or former spouse, and not if the Alternate Payee is a child or other dependent of the Participant. If the Alternate Payee is the Participant's spouse or former spouse, drafters may select sample paragraph 1, sample paragraph 2, or sample paragraph 3. Sample paragraph 1 applies if the Alternate Payee is treated as the Participant's spouse for all of the spousal survivor benefits payable with respect to the Participant's benefits under the Plan. Sample paragraph 2 applies if the Alternate Payee is treated as the Participant's spouse for a portion of the spousal survivor benefits payable with respect to the Participant's benefits under the Plan. Sample paragraph 3 applies if the Alternate Payee is not treated as the Participant's spouse for any of the spousal survivor benefits payable with respect to the Participant's benefits under the Plan.

1. Alternate Payee Treated as Spouse for All Spousal Survivor Benefits

(62) The Alternate Payee shall be treated as the Participant's spouse under the Plan for purposes of Sections 401(a)(11) and 417 of the Code.

2. Alternate Payee Treated as Spouse for a Portion of the Spousal Survivor Benefits

(63) The Alternate Payee shall be treated as the Participant's spouse under the Plan for purposes of Sections 401(a)(11) and 417 of the Code with respect to [insert percentage of benefit or a formula, such as a formula describing the benefit earned under the plan during marriage].

3. Alternate Payee Not Treated as Spouse

(64) The Alternate Payee shall not be treated as the Participant's spouse under the Plan.

Small Business Job Protection Act of 1996
H.R. 3448

Section 1457: Sample Language for Spousal Consent and Qualified Domestic Relations Forms

(a) **Development of sample language**—Not later than January 1, 1997, the Secretary of the Treasury shall develop—

(1) sample language for inclusion in a form for the spousal consent required under Section 417(a)(2) of the Internal Revenue Code of 1986 and Section 205(c)(2) of the Employee Retirement Income Security Act of 1974 which—

(A) is written in a manner calculated to be understood by the average person, and

(B) discloses in plain form—

(i) whether the waiver to which the spouse consents is irrevocable, and

(ii) whether such waiver may be revoked by a qualified domestic relations order, and

(2) sample language for inclusion in a form for a qualified domestic relations order described in Section 414(p)(1)(A) of such Code and Section 206(d)(3)(B)(i) of such Act which—

(A) meets the requirements contained in such sections, and

(B) the provisions of which focus attention on the need to consider the treatment of any lump sum payment, qualified joint and survivor annuity, or qualified preretirement survivor annuity.

(b) **Publicity**—The Secretary of the Treasury shall include publicity for the sample language developed under subsection (a) in the pension outreach efforts undertaken by the Secretary.

20. Treasury to provide model forms for spousal consent and qualified domestic relations orders (Sec. 1457 of the Senate Amendment).

Present Law

Present law contains a number of rules designed to provide income to the surviving spouse of a deceased employee. Under these spousal protection rules, defined benefit pension plans and money purchase pension plans are required to provide that vested retirement benefits with a present value in excess of $3,500 are payable in the form of a qualified joint and survivor annuity (QJSA) or in the case of a participant who dies before the annuity starting date, a qualified preretirement survivor annuity (QPSA). Benefits from a plan subject to the survivor benefit rules may be paid in a form other than a QJSA or QPSA if the participant waives the QJSA or QPSA (or both) and the applicable notice, election and spousal consent requirements are satisfied.

Also, under present law, benefits under a qualified retirement plan are subject to prohibitions against assignment or alienation of benefits. An exception to this rule generally applies in the case of plan benefits paid to a former spouse pursuant to a qualified domestic relations order (QDRO).

House Bill

No provision.

Senate Amendment

Model spousal consent form

The Secretary is required to develop a model spousal consent form, no later than January 1, 1997, waiving the QJSA and QPSA forms of benefit. Such form must be written in a manner calculated to be understood by the average person, and must disclose in plain form whether the waiver is irrevocable and that it may be revoked by a QDRO.

Model QDRO

The Secretary is required to develop a model QDRO, no later than January 1, 1997, which satisfies the requirements of a QDRO under present law, and the provisions of which focus attention on the need to consider the treatment of any lump sum payment, QJSA, or QPSA.

Effective Date

The provisions are effective on the date of enactment.

Conference Agreement

The conference agreement follows the Senate amendment, except that instead of developing a model spousal consent form and a model QDRO, the Secretary must develop sample language for inclusion in a spousal consent form and QDRO.

Articles

"A 12-Point Checklist to Weigh the Legitimacy of Your QDRO Claims," 94-4 *IOMA's Report on Managing 401(k) Plans*, 2 (1994).

"ABA Submits Report on QDROs," *Highlights and Documents*, 3439 (March 3, 1995).

Beam and Tacchino, "Employee Benefit Planning," 67 *Journal of the American Society of CLU and ChFC*, 8 (1993).

Boutwell, "Practical Advice on QDRO Quagmire," *Panel Publishers 401(k) Advisor*, 2 (March 1997).

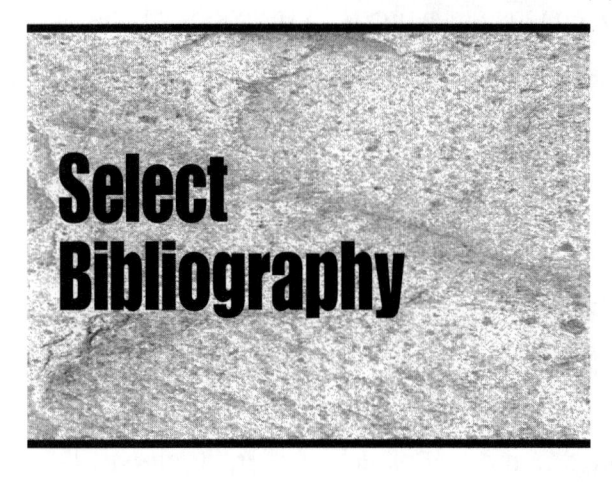

Brucker and Hiltunen, "The Firm Beware: When Non-ERISA Professionals Advise on Retirement Matters," 2 *Journal of Pension Benefits*, 80 (1995).

Churchill, "Qualified Domestic Relations Orders: Traps for the Unwary," 1 *Journal of Pension Benefits*, 9 (1994).

"Compliance With QDRO Rules Shifted Tax Burden on Qualified Plan Benefits to Ex-Spouse," *Pension and Benefits Week*, 9 (July 10, 1996).

Cook, "Qualified Domestic Relations Orders," 41 *Louisiana Bar Journal*, 420 (1994).

"Divorce and the Plan Administrator—Watch Those Procedures," *CCH Compliance Guide for Plan Administrators* (April 8, 1994).

Dodge and Morris, "QDROs and Welfare Benefit Plans After *Metropolitan Life v. Wheaton*," 8 *Benefits Law Journal*, 43 (1995).

Edmond and Landsman, "Do You or Don't You? The Nitty-Gritty on Domestic Relations Orders," 17 *Benefits and Compensation Journal*, 48 (1995).

"Established Procedures, Form Letters Keys to Successful QDRO Administration," *CCH Compliance Guide for Plan Administrators*, 214 (February 10, 1995).

Gross, "How to Ensure That a DRO Qualifies Under the Detailed Tax and ERISA Requirements," 81 *The Journal of Taxation*, 346 (1994).

International Foundation of Employee Benefit Plans, "Qualified Medical Child Support Orders (QMCSOs)," *Practices*, 2nd Quarter (1994).

MacMillan and Nebel, "The Dilemmas of Divorce," 73 *HR Focus*, 11 (1996).

Meyer, "Qualified Domestic Relations Orders: What the Statute Doesn't Say," 7 *Benefits Law Journal*, 311 (1994).

Murtha, "Divorce Is Hard on Benefit Managers," 12 *Crain's New York Business*, 22 (June 17, 1996).

Norquist, "Qualified Domestic Relations Orders: A Plan Administrator's Operational Perspective," 11 *Benefits Quarterly*, 76 (1995).

Perdue, "QDROs and Qualified Plan Rules Pose Problems for Fiduciaries and Participants," 3 *Journal of Taxation of Employee Benefits*, 71 (1995).

Potter, "How to Draft a Qualified Domestic Relations Order," 1 *Journal of Taxation of Employee Benefits*, 250 (1994).

"QDROs: Experts Say Rules Too Complex, Time-Consuming for Plan Administrators," 20 *BNA Pension Reporter News*, 2376 (1993).

Richardson, "Qualified Domestic Relations Orders: Navigating the Cross Fire," 11 *Compensation and Benefits Journal*, 48 (1995).

Shulman, "Your Client's Entitlement to Pension Benefits: Understanding QDROs," 6 *American Journal of Family Law*, 197 (1992).

Smith, "When Is a DRO a QDRO?" 19 *Employee Benefits Journal*, 37 (1994).

Westbrook, "Update on Qualified Domestic Relations Orders," 25 *The Pension Actuary*, 6 (1995).

Zimmerman, "Taxing Retirement Distributions at Divorce in the Absence of a Qualified Domestic Relations Order," 73 *Taxes*, 326 (1995).

Books

Bloss, *QDROs: A Guide for Plan Administration*, (1991).

Gucciardi and Knox, *Pension Distribution Answer Book: Special Supplement Forms and Worksheets*, (1997).

McCarthy, *Financial Planning for a Secure Retirement*, (1996).

Meyen and Dundee, *Qualified Domestic Relations Order Answer Book*, (1996).

Moss, *Your Pension Rights at Divorce: What Women Need to Know*, (1991, rev. 1995).

PBGC, *Divorce Orders and PBGC*, (1996).

Shulman, *Qualified Domestic Relations Orders Handbook*, (1993).

Snyder, *Financial Issues in Divorce—Qualified Domestic Relations Orders*, (1993).

Resources on the Internet

Benefits and Human Resources

BENEFITS-L Internet Resource Document
http://www.mtsu.edu/~rlhannah/employee_benefits.html

BenefitsLink
http://www.benefitslink.com

International Foundation of Employee Benefit Plans
http://www.ifebp.org

Government

Department of Labor (DOL)
http://www.dol.gov

Internal Revenue Service (IRS)
http://www.irs.ustreas.gov

PBGC Pension Search Directory
http://search.pbgc.gov

Pension and Welfare Benefits Administration (PWBA)
http://www.dol.gov/dol/pwba

Pension Benefit Guaranty Corporation (PBGC)
http://www.pbgc.gov

Legal

Code of Federal Regulations
http://law.house.gov/cfr.htm

The Practicing Attorney's Home Page
http://www.legalethics.com/pa

Supreme Court Decisions
http://www.law.cornell.edu/supct

U.S. House of Representatives Internet Law Library
http://law.house.gov

PLEASE NOTE: *This information does not constitute an endorsement by the International Foundation of Employee Benefit Plans of any of the entities or individuals sponsoring the listed WorldWide Web sites.*

Alternate payees, 10-11, 28

Beneficiary
rights of, 23-24
Benefits
freezing of, 29-30
payment of, 12-13
Burton v. Commissioner, 37-38

Checklist *see* Qualified domestic relations orders (QDROs) checklists for
Claims
release form samples, 32-34
releasing claim to retirement benefits, 31
COBRA *see* Consolidated Omnibus Budget Reconciliation Act (COBRA)
Communication
approaches to, 43-45
internal, 76
optional, 53-55
required by law, 45-46
sample letters, 47-52
sample packet for, 55-66
simplification of, 79
see also Qualified domestic relations orders (QDROs) communication
Consent form (sample), 66
Consolidated Omnibus Budget Reconciliation Act (COBRA)
plans subject to, 6-7

Divorce file cover sheet (sample), 73
DOL *see* Department of Labor (DOL)

Domestic relations order (DRO)
    legal requirements for, 9-10
Department of Labor (DOL)
    questions for, 2, 9-10
Department of Labor (DOL) Advisory Opinion 94-32A, 75-76
DRO *see* domestic relations order (DRO)

Employee Retirement Income Security Act of 1974 (ERISA), 1, 2, 5, 10, 23, 26, 75, 76
ERISA Section 206(d)(3)
    text, 90-94
ERISA *see* Employee Retirement Income Security Act of 1974 (ERISA)

Fiduciary duties, 22-23

Hawkins v. Commissioner, 36-37
Hopkins v. AT&T Global Information Solutions Inc., 29-30

Internal Revenue Code (IRC)
    section 401(a)(11), 13
    section 401(a)(13), 5
    section 414(p), 5, 8
    section 414(p) text, 85-89
    section 417, 13
IRC *see* Internal Revenue Code (IRC)
IRS Notice 97-11 (sample language for a qualified domestic relations order), 21
    appendix to, 109-121
    text of, 105-109
    treasury guidance, 3

Karem v. Commissioner, 37

Lynn v. Lynn, 23-24

Managing QDROs, 69-84
    distribution restrictions, 70-71
    paperwork organization, 71-72
    procedures needed, 69-70
Metropolitan Life v. Wheaton, 5, 6

Names and mailing addresses
    clear specification of, 11-12
Notice 97-11 *see* IRS Notice 97-11
Notification of QDRO approval (sample), 50
Notification that order is not a QDRO, no assistance offered (sample), 51
Notification that order is not a QDRO, offering assistance (sample), 52

Orders *see* Domestic relations order (DRO) legal requirements for

Plan administrators
    legal obligations of, 19-42
Plan information
    beneficiary rights, 23-24
    burdensome requests for, 28
    fiduciary duties, 22-23
    general information, 26-27
    privacy concerns, 22-23
    release of, 22-28
    subpoenas, 24-26
    two participants, 26
    valuation issues, 27-28
Plan language, 8-9
Privacy concerns *see* Plan information privacy concerns

Procedures
  documenting, 20-21
  establishing, 19-20
  sample language for, 21-22

QDROs *see* Qualified domestic relations orders (QDROs)
QDRO order (sample), 35
QMCSOs *see* Qualified medical child support orders (QMCSOs)
Qualified domestic relations orders (QDROs)
  background, 1-2
  checklists for, 13-14, 62-63
  communication, 43-68
  definition of, 4
  determining status of, 35-36
  fees for, 74-76
  information collection, 35-36
  legal requirements for, 9-13
  management of, 69-72
  sample of, 64-65
  tax consequences of, 36-39
  types of, 4-8
Qualified medical child support orders (QMCSOs)
  plans subject to, 6-7

REA *see* Retirement Equity Act of 1984 (REA)
Release of plan information *see* Plan information release of
Retirement Equity Act of 1984 (REA), 1, 5, 6
  text of legislative history, 98-104
Retirement plans, 7-8

Sample consent form, 66
Sample language
  procedures for determination of QDROs, 21-22
Sample letters
  acknowledges claim from spouse of plan participant, 56
  acknowledges receipt of order and describes QDRO determination procedures, 49
  advises participant that order is not a QDRO—offers assistance, 52
  advises participant that order is not a QDRO—offers no assistance, 51
  notifies participant and alternate payee of approval of order as a QDRO, 50
Sample memos
  answers frequently asked questions, 57-58
  assistance to other employees in processing a QDRO, 80
  confirmation of approved QDRO and instructions for assignment, 83
  confirmation of receipt of notice of pending divorce, 82
  documentation of telephone conversations, 81
  response to divorce attorneys, 59-61
  response to routine inquiries about divorce, 77-78
Sample QDRO, 64-65
Sample QDRO communications packet, 55-66

Index 131

Sample release forms
   release before DRO is QDRO, 32
   release to retirement account—no immediate distribution anticipated, 34
   release while divorce is pending, 33
SBJPA *see* Small Business Job Protection Act of 1996 (SBJPA)
Schoonmaker v. Employee Savings Plan of Amoco Corp., 30-31
Segregated accounts, 20
Selecting and training personnel, 76

Shelstead v. Shelstead, 11-12
Small Business Job Protection Act of 1996 (SBJPA), 3
   text relating to QDROs, 122-123
Subpoenas, 24-26

Tax consequences, 36-39
Treasury guidance, 3-4
Treasury Regulation Section 1.401(a)-13(g)
   text of, 95-97

Valuation issues, 27-28